All Together Now!

40 ready-to-use outlines for all-age worship

Compiled by Christine Wright

With grateful thanks to all the writers of SALT All-ages over the years, and in particular to Peter Graystone, who wrote the majority of this material. Without their creativity and commitment to resourcing an all-age church, this book could not have been produced.

Scripture Union, 207-209 Queensway, Bletchley, MK2 2EB, England.

© Scripture Union, 2000.

ISBN 1 85999 337 0

British Library Cataloguing-in-Publication Data A catalogue record for this book is available from the British Library.

Cover design by David Lund Design. Internal design by pre design consultants ltd. Illustrations by Pauline Adams.

Printed and bound in Malta by Interprint Ltd.

SALT For All ages

SALT is Scripture Union's quarterly programme which invites people of all ages to join together in exploring and responding to God's word in the Bible and to grow in their relationship with Jesus. Scripture Union recognises that every church situation is different and that children and adults think and learn in different ways, so there is a wide range of activities to choose from. Simply select from the clearly laid out options to create a balanced service or children's session from scratch, or enhance an outline you already have.

SALT for All ages is particularly adaptable. Each week's material forms the basis of an all-age service and enables the whole church to come together for all or part of the service to share worship and learning in a lively and engaging way. It includes sermon outlines and suggestions for worship and also provides resources for churches using the Revised (or Common Worship) Lectionary.

SALT for All ages is priced at £5.99 per quarter and can be obtained from Christian bookshops or from Scripture Union Mail Order, PO Box 5148, Milton Keynes MLO, MK2 2YX Tel: 01908 856006 Fax: 01908 856020.

contents

introduction

This book contains forty outlines for all-age worship. Some follow the church year and provide resources for its main seasons. In the second section, there are services suitable for all ages on important Christian themes which run through the Bible. You will find ideas for Remembrance Sunday at the back of the book.

Why have all-age worship?
It's biblical practice!
Look in the Old Testament and see how much 'worship' took place in the community with children obviously being part of all that was going on. When the people of Israel were given instructions about how to treat children, there is no mention of 'Sabbath-school' or the segregation of youngsters either in regular worship or at the great festivals. Their place was in the worshipping community and in the home which was where the vast majority of 'religious education' was taking place. Of course, there was no provision made for the children from homes where God was not acknowledged and Israelites had no sense of responsibility for anyone outside their own faith community. That may be one of the big differences between Old Testament times and our own at the beginning of the third millennium after Christ.

In New Testament times, the early church was more concerned for non-believers than the Jewish community had ever been. However, the apostles did not run holiday clubs, mid-week clubs and Sunday groups for children. Their evangelistic efforts went into adults, not because they did not care for children, but because they knew that once adults believed in Christ, the children would become part of the Christian community also and grow up immersed in all the activities of the church, including worship.

In our own time, society is very different. We cannot simply go back to the Bible and assume that whatever the early church did, we ought to be doing. (For instance, early Gentile believers invested a lot of time debating whether it was right for Christians to eat food offered to idols. I don't remember a single point on this matter ever being raised at a meeting in my own church! It simply isn't an issue for most of us.)

On the other hand, when it comes to very important matters such as how to nurture children from both Christian and non-Christian homes, we need to consider how much of what we regard as traditional Christian practice is in fact fairly recent.

During the past two centuries, while compulsory education for all children has been developing, there has been an assumption that children are best taught separately from adults. This has had some great benefits, especially when those working with children have used methods of teaching and nurturing especially adapted to the age and experience of their groups. Sadly, at the same time, in some traditions, adult worship and learning has been less rich, less colourful, less participative and more verbal and propositional.

How do you do all-age worship?
There is now a move to incorporate children back into mainstream worship (though age-related groups still have an important role). Being used to segregated worship and learning, church leaders have sometimes asked the following questions:
• How can we add something to our normal adult worship to make it more bearable for the children (for example, by having a few action songs)?
• How can we adapt children's worship to make it bearable for adults (for example, by adding an adult sermon but making it shorter)?
• How can we simplify the verbal teaching which we use with adults (for example, by having a sermon, but using visual aids)?
• How can we 'dumb down' adult worship so that the children understand everything that is going on?

All of these are the wrong questions! Instead we should be asking:
• How can we devise worship suitable for both children and adults together?
• How can we encourage adults to learn and worship in ways which are

simpler, but not at all shallow?
• How can we help children feel included at all stages without making our worship childish (and therefore embarrassing to everyone, including children)?

If we return to the idea of nurture rather than teaching, we may be able to answer some of these questions, but it does mean a shift in our thinking. Children (and adults, in fact!) learn not only from words, but from observing, participating, from atmosphere and from belonging. They learn and grow in faith by being included as equals in the worship of God. They may not 'understand' every word and every action (how many adults do?), but what they absorb from all that is happening around them will stay with them for life. All-age worship is neither adult worship for children, nor children's worship for adults. It is something different altogether!

What is all-age worship?

In their book *A Church for All Ages* (Scripture Union), Eileen Turner and Peter Graystone cite four principles for all-age worship:
1 It is *simple* - not simplistic, not boringly repetitive, not too obvious but straightforward and engaging for all - regardless of age. It has to be significant - based on issues which affect young and old alike - and these themes must be treated carefully so that, beyond the simplicity, there is more that will be

grasped by those who are open to it.
2 It is *not childish* - not embarrassing, not patronising, not silly. We all need to come before God as we are in our need of forgiveness, help and growth in faith. If we come pretending to be children, we cannot encounter God. We must be prepared to engage with God fully and honestly in all-age worship as with any other kind of worship.
3 It is *visual* where possible - or aural (not only verbal), tasty, smelly (in the nicest way), or tactile. Remember that young children cannot read and if the only visual aids are written words, however cleverly delivered, the youngest in the congregation will not be able to participate. 'The best visual aid is the real thing,' my college lecturer used to say. It is not necessary to spend hours and hours preparing a visual aid which will only last for a few seconds. Instead, think visually (and about using the other senses), asking yourself, 'What could I use to communicate with a child who can't read easily nor understand abstract statements?'
4 It is *interactive* where possible - and not only between the worship leader and the congregation. Being all ages together provides a wonderful opportunity for different generations to learn from each other and to get to know one another. It is not necessary or desirable for everything to be interactive. There also needs to be time for quiet reflection and activities which direct

the congregation God-ward. Interaction, however, ensures that no one leaves the service without being acknowledged and affirmed.

How to use this book

Arranging all-age worship is hard work, but it is very rewarding. There is much to consider, including the need to provide a full 'diet' of worship in each service (for instance, for confession and receiving of pardon, thanksgiving and praise, praying for others, learning, reflection, sending out and blessing the congregation).

This book provides ideas to help you on your way, but in no sense will any of the outlines provide all you need. Rather they are like the shelves of a supermarket from which you choose ingredients. You will then need to 'take them home' and add other ingredients from your store cupboard, decide how to combine them and finally how to present the dish to the family.

Apart from the nativity services which are written almost in full, the outlines are set out under the following headlines:

Service title

The title is a 'headline' giving a glimpse of what follows.

Bible theme/Christian theme

An at-a-glance picture of where the service fits in terms of the church

year or the broad scheme of Christian thought.

Bible base

The Bible passages to be studied and explored during the service.

All-age service summary

A quick overview of how the theme will be presented.

This week's resources

Advice about how to use the resources and any important things to be prepared or considered before beginning.

Setting the scene

An idea for how to open up the theme, beginning with something that everyone will already know about or understand. This section is designed to interest and/or intrigue the congregation about the theme of the service.

Bible reading

Suggestions for different ways of presenting the Bible reading(s).

Bible teaching for all ages

This section is not simply about words and ideas to which the congregation will listen. It provides a mixture of ways in which Bible teaching can be given which will interest and engage everyone.

Ideas for music

There are so many hymn and song books that no attempt has been made to identify in which books the hymns or songs can be found. If you do not recognise the first-line titles of any item, look for something more familiar on the theme which this section suggests.

Prayers

The 'prayer' section contains different ways of praying and many different styles and kinds of prayer. Remember that short or participatory prayers are just as meaningful as long or single-voice prayers and much more suitable for children who have a shorter attention span than adults.

And finally...

Leading all-age worship demands a certain amount of courage. Allowing greater participation involves an element of risk! The leader is not totally in control of what may be said or what may happen and opens up the possibility that things may not go according to plan. On the other hand, good all-age worship allows for fun and spontaneity and provides new ways in which God can speak to anyone and everyone as they meet to worship. It's a risk well worth taking.

Extra!

As older and younger members of the congregation get to know one another, you may find that it's a good idea to arrange some social events which bring all ages together. So many of our church activities are age-segregated so that 'church' appears not to be 'family' at all. Bringing everyone together to enjoy each other's company is an expression of our essential oneness in Christ. For those on the fringe of the church community, such 'low-threat' events could be the means by which they are drawn in closer - an opportunity to feel what it is like to belong. This could be an important step in their growth towards God.

Some ideas for fun together

These ideas can be used at any time of the year when an event is planned for all ages together. Resist the urge to invite only children! There is enormous value in encouraging different generations to enjoy themselves with one another.

A picnic

Choose a local place of interest or a beauty spot. Arrange transport for anyone who needs it. Ask everyone to bring food and drink for themselves, plus a small extra amount in case anyone forgets their own. Plan activities which could involve anyone (ball games tend to attract some people and bore others) like parachute (play canopy) games, a simple treasure hunt, a collecting game ('Find five stones of different colours, three different kinds of leaves, something red', etc) or games which will involve talking to one another ('Find two people with the same initials, someone who remembers what they were doing when John F Kennedy was shot, someone who has had less than five birthdays', etc).

A fun afternoon

Arrange for several craft-type activities to be available for people to try. As an example, there could be painting, modelling clay, carpentry, cookery, construction (Lego or similar), simple scientific experiments, lace-making, crochet, stone polishing (or whatever else people can offer). The idea is to dabble for a while in lots of different hobbies, not to achieve masterpieces, but who knows what talents will be realised? Invite both young and old to take part, moving from table to table as they wish. Provide refreshments (ice-cream, or home-made cakes?) and close with everyone together listening to a well-told story or singing some favourite songs.

Games evening

People of all ages love board games and most households will have at least one. A get-together to play and learn board games could be easily arranged, with an area set aside for the youngest children and their toys.

Water carrying

This idea has a more serious objective, but can still be great fun. In some countries, people (often women and children) have to walk long distances to find water and then carry it home. Challenge those who are able to do so, to walk together to collect water in buckets and bring it back to a central meeting place. Water could be collected from a stream, river, lake, reservoir or canal. (A similar walk to the tap in someone's kitchen would do if another source of water is unavailable!) The object is for people to experience walking at least a mile, preferably a little more, carrying water. It's much harder than most of us would expect. Rewards could be given to those who manage to arrive with most water. A simple meal could then be shared, perhaps prepared by those not able to walk far - reflecting the cuisine of a country in which collecting water is a daily chore.

Bright and beautiful party

The theme of the party is based around the hymn 'All things bright and beautiful'. The idea is for groups each to make a poster or display depicting words from the hymn. For instance:
'All creatures great and small';
'The purple-headed mountain, the river running by';
'The ripe fruit in the garden'
The cold wind in the winter, the pleasant summer sun, etc
'He gave us eyes... and lips...'
Provide a simple meal (always a crowd-puller!) and conclude by singing the hymn and listening to words from Psalm 8 or Psalm 104.

One group could be asked to find a creative way of presenting the chosen verses with slides or movement. (This idea is a great antidote to Hallowe'en parties.)

For other ideas see:

John Hattam, *Families Finding Faith* (Scripture Union/CPAS, £7.50)
John Marshall, *The Bumper Book of Family Activities* (Scripture Union, £4.95).

As writer and editor, Christine Wright has been involved in producing Scripture Union's church resources for over twenty years. She is now a freelance writer and editor, living in and enjoying the Buckinghamshire countryside.

advent sunday

advent sunday

OUTLINE 1

SERVICE THEME
Jesus Christ – yet to come

CHURCH YEAR
Advent Sunday

BIBLE BASE
Acts 1:1–11

ALL-AGE SERVICE SUMMARY
The service looks forward to the return of Jesus and recognises that when he returned to heaven, he gave his followers work to do until he comes again.

THIS WEEK'S RESOURCES
Create your all-age service by choosing from these resources and arranging them to suit your own situation.

Setting the scene

Remark that you have seen advent calendars in the shops and ask who has one at home, ready to open the first window (or with the first few open). Produce your own large home-made Advent calendar with six windows (as shown in the illustration on page 8). Invite six children to open the windows in order. When they are all open, they reveal the word 'coming'. That is what the word 'Advent' means. It refers to the fact that Christmas is coming, and the calendar helps us keep track of the days passing so that we will not only be ready with the decorations, presents and food, but also be ready to worship Jesus who came to earth as a human baby. However, it also refers to another coming - the time when Jesus will come back to our planet to put right everything that is wrong, and to live gloriously with his followers for ever. Both these 'comings' are things that Christians look forward to joyfully.

Bible reading
Acts 1:1–11

Explain before the reading that Luke is writing a book for his friend Theophilus. Already he has written a book about all that Jesus did from his birth in Bethlehem until his death and resurrection. Now he is writing about what happened next...

Bible teaching for all ages

Photocopy enough copies of the illustration on page 8 for everyone (or perhaps every family group or group of friends) to have one. At the beginning of the talk, show the congregation how to fold the sheets forward along the vertical line in the centre, then back along the lines on the right. This should reveal two pictures: one in which Jesus is speaking and one in which the men in white appear.

Ask everyone to hold the picture firstly in the position where Jesus can be seen. Describe what happened in Acts 1:4-8. Explain that now Jesus has returned to heaven, we are to be his witnesses. We are to carry on the work that he did on earth, and the Holy Spirit will help us do so. Invite the congregation to think about what kinds of things Jesus wants us to do for him, now that he is doing his work through *our* hands and spreading his good news through *our* mouths. Suggest that they talk to those sitting next to them about their ideas and write or draw some answers in the box.

Then ask everyone to fold the flap across to reveal the second picture. Continue the story as it is told in Acts 1:9-11. Talk about Jesus' return, and how much Christians look forward to it because it will bring an end to all that is wrong in our world. We do not know when it will be, so Jesus asks us to be ready and doing his work (including the things that have been written or drawn) in preparation for that day.

Ideas for music

Choose songs and hymns which focus on the continuation of Jesus' work through his church/followers. Examples:
'At the name of Jesus'
'Mighty in victory'
'Swing wide the gates'
'I want to serve the purpose of God'
'There is a Redeemer'
'The Servant King'
'When Jesus moved beyond our sight'
'When the King shall come again'
'Great is the darkness that covers the earth'

Prayers
Maranatha prayer
Come, Lord Jesus, to put an end to all that grieves the heart of God. Come…
Come, Lord Jesus.
To end the domination that disadvantages women and children and favours men, come…
Come, Lord Jesus.
To end the suffering of innocent people when humans take up arms against one another, come…
Come, Lord Jesus.
To end the shame of lives trapped in poverty while the rich flaunt their wealth, come…
Come, Lord Jesus.
To end the plight of those with no home, no country, or no hope, come…

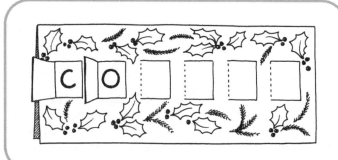

Come, Lord Jesus.
To end the fear of those who have no one but you to turn to, come...
Come, Lord Jesus.
To end the sadness of those parted by death from those they love, come...
Come, Lord Jesus. Amen.

Being ready
Say this poem rhythmically, the congregation responding to the leader, having first established the rhythm by clicking fingers.

Jesus is coming.
Let's get ready.
Maybe this year.
Let's get ready.
Maybe ten years.
Let's get ready.
Maybe thousands.
Let's get ready.
No more fighting.

Let's get ready.
No more hating.
Let's get ready.
No more hurting.
Let's get ready.
Gotta tell your neighbours.
Let's get ready.
Gotta tell your school friends.
Let's get ready.
Gotta tell the whole world.
Let's get ready.
Gonna be amazing!
Let's get ready.

Doing Jesus' work
After the Bible teaching, invite some people to tell everyone what they drew or wrote in their boxes. When several things have been mentioned, the leader should combine them as a prayer, or an open time of prayer could be held asking God the Holy Spirit to strengthen us to do these things.

Intercessions
Remember in prayer any who have been commissioned by your church for service as missionaries, then go on to pray for places in the world where injustice or unhappiness have featured in the news, perhaps copying headlines on to overhead projector acetates to give a visual focus.

Being witnesses
As people leave the service, give them balloons to take away with them, on which are written the words: 'Jesus is coming back'. This could be a way (both symbolically and literally) of taking the message to the neighbourhood.

advent sunday

---

advent sun

OUTLINE 2

SERVICE THEME
Jesus is coming - get ready!

CHURCH YEAR
Advent Sunday

BIBLE BASE
Luke 1:26-38 with Isaiah 11:1-9 as a complementary reading

ALL-AGE SERVICE SUMMARY
Unwrapping the dual meaning of Advent Sunday - a reminder that it is time not only to prepare for Christmas (God's promise to Mary of a son), but also that it is time to prepare ourselves for the second coming of Christ by doing the work he wants us to do and by being at peace with God.

THIS WEEK'S RESOURCES
Create your all-age service by choosing from these resources and arranging them to suit your own situation. Omit Isaiah 11:1-9 if you have a high proportion of very young children.

Setting the scene
Describe or even better play (perhaps with a couple of young children and their parents or carers) a game of hide and seek. Draw attention to the moment when, having counted down from one hundred to one, the seeker calls out, 'Coming, ready or not!'

Today is Advent Sunday, the time when everybody is looking forward to what *we* are looking forward to. For many people, it is the time they start looking forward to Christmas. Certainly for Mary, about whom everyone will hear today, there was one particular memorable day when she knew she had to start getting ready for her baby to be born. But for Christians it is a time when we think about the fact that Jesus will return to earth one day.

In fact, 'Coming, ready or not!' is what Jesus says to us at this time of year. It is almost as if he is asking us to be prepared for him to come and seek us out. He wants us to be prepared - *in our hearts*, by knowing that we can meet him with sins forgiven and at peace with God; *and in our lives* by doing the work he would have us do to make the world in a fit state to receive him. It's time to start getting ready for Christmas; but it's also time to be getting ready to meet Jesus face to face.

Bible readings
Luke 1:26-38
This could be read using a narrator and two voices, one male (reading the angel's words) and the other a young woman or older girl (reading Mary's words).
Isaiah 11:1-9
If this reading is used, use two readers with contrasting voices. Most verses in this passage divide naturally into two phrases. Verse 5 could be read by both readers in unison.

Bible teaching for all ages
Prepare for this talk by making a large clock from two pieces of card. The diagram overleaf shows how to construct it. When the dial is turned, the following three headings are made to appear:

Mary's time had come
Gabriel appeared to Mary telling her that she would have a baby. It was no ordinary baby. People would call him 'Son of the Most High' (Luke 1:32). This baby would grow up to be the King of a kingdom that would last forever. It was time for Jesus to come into the world.

Messiah's time would come
Mary was not the first to know that Jesus would be born. A long time ago, God's special people, the Jews, began waiting for their leader to be born. They called him the Messiah. The prophet Isaiah told them about the kingdom which he would set up (11:1-9):
1 It would be a kingdom where the King worked on behalf of poor people instead of spending all his time with the rich.
2 A kingdom where the King made sure that decisions were made fairly; and where those who cheat, do wrong, or where people who become successful by making others fail, are punished.
3 A kingdom where the King turned his back on going to war and did everything he could to make peace between people.
It was time for Jesus to be revealed as the Messiah.

Our time has come
Jesus lived and died, was raised to life and returned to heaven. He has set up his kingdom and now we are waiting for the time which will surely come, when he will return to make it perfect. While we are waiting, God expects us to be doing the work that Jesus started:
1) Making peace between people.
2) Making sure that the poor are treated fairly.
3) Helping those who are in need.
It is time for us to be doing Jesus' work, showing people what the kingdom of God is like.
Afterwards, ask the congregation to suggest some of the ways in which the church is already active in these three areas - and perhaps ask for ideas of new ways of doing this work. This can be done first in small groups and then receive a few answers with everyone listening. As a visual reminder, place in a row

where everyone can see them, a clock or watch after each one of these answers. Ask the questions carefully so that children can contribute, eg 'How do we as Christians help to make peace between people - at home, at school, at work, in our town?'

Ideas for music

Choose songs and hymns which reflect the kingship of Jesus, the expectation of Christ's coming or the work of peacemaking, justice and caring.
Examples:
'Lift up your heads to the coming king'
'Meekness and majesty
'My peace I give to you'
'O come, o come Emmanuel'
'Soon and very soon'
'Men of faith, rise up and sing'
'Lord I lift your name on high' *('You came from heaven to earth')*
'This child'

Prayers
To be more like Jesus
A prayer based on Isaiah 11:2-5

Jesus is filled with the Spirit of God,
Jesus, make us more like you.
Jesus knows what the Lord's will is for him,
Jesus, make us more like you.
Jesus takes pleasure in obeying his Father,
Jesus, make us more like you.
Jesus does not judge people by outward appearance,
Jesus, make us more like you.
Jesus wants justice for all who are poor,
Jesus, make us more like you.
Jesus defends the rights of the helpless,
Jesus, make us more like you.
Jesus has come to bring peace between people,
Jesus, make us more like you.
Jesus is King and we are his people,
Jesus, make us more like you.
Amen.

A prayer of confession
Invite the congregation to cluster into groups of three or four, adults and children together, by turning on the seats or pews. Ask them to talk together and make a list of things that Jesus would be disappointed to see us doing when he returns (remind adults not to make their contributions childish). After a minute or two, invite some to suggest what they decided. The leader should then say a prayer asking for forgiveness, mentioning the congregation's suggestions. Next ask the groups to consider what Jesus would be pleased to see us doing when he comes back. After hearing suggestions as before, the leader should pray that we will be ready to serve Jesus in these ways, doing the work of the King whenever there is a need.

A prayer of longing
Use these words of a Negro spiritual, spoken rhythmically by the leader with the congregation responding. A drum rhythm in the background would add to its impact.

Lord, I want to be a Christian,
In my heart, in my heart,
Lord I want to be a Christian,
In my heart.

Lord, I want to be more loving,
In my heart, in my heart,
Lord, I want to be more loving,
In my heart.

Lord, I want to be like Jesus,
In my heart, in my heart,
Lord, I want to be like Jesus,
In my heart.

Closing prayer
Words of Hartich Sierck, a middle-European peasant, in 1628:

God send that there may be an end at last;
God send that there may be peace again;
God in heaven, send us peace. Amen.

An advent clock

An advent clock

advent sunday

OUTLINE 3

SERVICE THEME
How to be rich and yet own nothing

CHURCH YEAR
Advent Sunday

BIBLE BASE
Matthew 19:16-30 with Isaiah 60:1-3,18-20 as a complementary reading

ALL-AGE SERVICE SUMMARY
Using the gospel story of a rich young man who wanted to follow Jesus, the service looks forward to the coming of Christ and focuses on priorities for Christian living as we wait and work for the fulfilment of the kingdom of heaven.

THIS WEEK'S RESOURCES
Create your all-age service by choosing from these resources and arranging them to suit your own situation. The drama, though not an essential part of the service, makes the point both clearly and visually.

Advent prayer

These words looking forward to the coming of Christ are from Isaiah 60:1-3,18-20. Every time the word 'light' comes in the reading, the congregation responds, 'Shine, Jesus, shine'. A hand movement to accompany this involves fingers spreading like a star-burst three times. The prayer could be used in conjunction with lighting the first candle of an Advent wreath.
This activity leads naturally into singing, 'Lord, the light of your love is shining'.

Arise, shine, for your light...
Shine, Jesus, shine.
...has come, and the glory of the Lord rises upon you. See, darkness covers the earth and thick darkness is over the peoples, but the Lord rises upon you and his glory appears over you. Nations will come to your light...
Shine, Jesus, shine.
...and kings to the brightness of your dawn ... No longer will violence be heard in your land, nor ruin or destruction within your borders, but you will call your walls Salvation and your gates Praise. The sun will no more be your light...
Shine, Jesus, shine.
...by day, nor will the brightness of the moon shine on you, for the Lord will be your everlasting light...
Shine, Jesus, shine.
...and your God will be your glory. Your sun will never set again, and your moon will wane no more; the Lord will be your everlasting light...
Shine, Jesus, shine.
...and your days of sorrow will end.

Setting the scene

Why light a candle at Advent? In years gone by, before every street was filled with electric light, people used to light a candle and place it in the window of a house so that travellers coming home on a dark night would know which way to go in the dark. Sometimes one of the household would have to go away for a long time - perhaps because he had to serve in the army or go on a sea voyage. Then a candle would be kept alight all the time he was gone as a sign of hope and expectation that he would return.

Well, Jesus has gone to his Father in heaven with a promise that he will return to take us there with him. He has kept every other promise, so Christians are confident that he will keep this one. On Advent Sunday, let's light a candle as a symbol of our hope and expectation that one day we will be welcoming Jesus back to our world.

In the meantime, we have work to do to prepare ourselves. A candle can also be a sign to us that light is better than darkness, that good is better than evil, that joy is better than despair, that generosity is better than selfishness, and that serving God is better than serving money.

In today's story, a man asked Jesus what he had to do in order to live with him forever in eternal life. Jesus' answer took him by surprise. He talked about the way to prepare yourself for heaven. It was challenging stuff. It still is.

Bible reading

Matthew 19:16-26
This reading lends itself well to a setting for three readers - a narrator (who can leave out short pieces of connecting text such as, 'He said'), the young man and Jesus.

Drama

All yours!
Characters: God's voice; man or woman.
There are no props; all are mimed. The man or woman stands in the centre and responds to the voice he or she hears, which seems to come from above and to the right.
Voice: *(Calls out the person's real name.)*
Person: Yes, Lord!
Voice: So when you said you wanted to follow me, were you really serious?
Person: Oh yes, Lord! Whatever you ask! I'm ready to give everything.
Voice: I see. Well, what about the new microwave you've just bought?
Person: What about it?
Voice: You said you wanted to give everything to me, but you're keeping that for yourself.
Person: Oh Lord, do I have to give that to you? It cooks baked potatoes in four minutes!

Voice: I thought you were serious!

Person: I am serious. It's yours. Here it is. *(Goes to the left, picks up an imaginary package, carries it to the right and puts it down.)* OK now?

Voice: Well, what about your music system?

Person: Do you really want my CD player?

Voice: Look, I thought you were serious about surrendering all!

Person: Lord, I love that system. All right. For you! *(Mimes moving a package as before, but a much heavier one.)* OK?

Voice: I think you're getting the idea. But what about your car? Are you hanging on to that or are you giving that to me too?

Person: How am I going to get to church? To work?

Voice: Serious or not?

Person: *(Thoughtful pause.)* Here it is. *(Mimes pushing the car across from left to right. It takes a lot of effort.)*

Voice: You're getting better. But there's more. What about the flat you live in? Is that going to belong to me?

Person: What, the very roof over my head?

Voice: The very roof over your head.

Person: *(Swallows hard.)* All right, Lord. *(Puts shoulder against the imaginary building and pushes. It won't budge.)* You're going to have to come and help me. *(Inch by inch, it moves.)* There you are. That's everything - the microwave, the CD player, the car, the flat. I'm just left here with the clothes I'm standing up in. *(There is a pause, during which the character's face shows that it's registering that even they have to go and then gives a long moan.)* No! O Lord, you make things so difficult. *(Mimes ripping off his outer clothes and throwing them to the right crossly.)* Here you are. You've got everything now. I'm just left here in my underwear and... *(A dreadful thought suddenly occurs to the character who looks up, grimacing and petulantly mimes taking them*

off and throwing them offstage.)* You've got the lot! I hope you're satisfied.

Voice: *(Pause, then gently calls the character's name. The character pretends not to listen. The voice calls again.)*

Person: *(Reluctantly.)* Yes.

Voice: You can have your clothes back.

Person: *(Scrambles back into them.)* Oh thank you, thank you.

Voice: But there's a condition. This is it. If you see anyone around you - in the church, in your street, on the news - who needs clothes that you have, you are to give them to them. Do you understand?

Person: *(Beginning to see.)* Ah, yes Lord! That's fine.

Voice: And you can have your flat back because I want you to have somewhere to live. But there's a condition! If anyone you know is suddenly short of somewhere to stay, or if anyone in church needs to hold a meeting and you've got an empty room that's right for it, that room is to be made available to them. Do you understand?

Person: Yes, Lord. I'm beginning to see. So although I seem to own it, I'm really managing it on your behalf. You own it, and I use it in a way that pleases you.

Voice: Well done! You're getting the idea! And here's your car back as well. But there's a condition. If anyone needs a lift anywhere, if anyone needs to borrow a car, if you can make that car useful in any way, then it becomes mine to be used on my behalf.

Person: *(Mimes receiving back his possessions one by one.)* Thank you, Lord, that's just fine.

Voice: And here's your stereo back. And here's your microwave back. But the same things apply. You can even have some CDs to go with it. You can go out to restaurants once in a while, and you can go on good holidays, because I want you to enjoy my world! But whenever those things are needed for my work

among children, women and men, then they are mine.

Person: Yes Lord, I understand. That's good. That's very good.

Voice: And *(name)*.

Person: *(Quietly.)* Yes.

Voice: I love you very much.

Person: *(Pause.)* I love you too.

Bible teaching for all ages

Show the picture of a hot-air balloon (see page 13). (Alternatively, you could use a home-made one made out of a helium balloon with a paper basket attached by strings.) Imagine you are floating in a hot-air balloon somewhere over the mountains. There are spectacular views! And in the balloon with you is everything you own. (OK, so it's a big balloon!)

Suddenly you realise that there is a puncture and the air which keeps the balloon aloft is leaking out of it. Nothing can be done to patch it - the only alternative is to start throwing possessions out in order to make the balloon lighter and keep it afloat. All our friends, family and pets are safe, so don't worry about them. But you can only keep one possession. What would it be? After a moment to think about it, invite the congregation to turn to the two or three people next to them, and tell them what object they have decided to keep - and why. After a couple of minutes, regain the congregation's attention and ask whether two or three people would like to tell everyone what they chose. (Pick a cross-section of adults and children to contribute. Keep this full of fun!)

Today's Bible reading was about a man who met Jesus and was put on the spot. Would he give up the things which were most precious to him in order to go with Jesus? As happens so often in life, this story did not have the expected happy ending.

Jesus said some tough things! Read Matthew 19:21. Following him

is not something to take lightly. It doesn't just mean finding time to think about him; it means spending all your time living in a way he would want. It doesn't just mean giving money to God's work; it means making all your money and possessions available for his work.

Like the rich man in the story, those who find it hardest to hand things over to God's use are often those who have most. No wonder Jesus said it was like a camel trying to squeeze through the eye of a needle. Impossible! So how can a rich person go to heaven? Not by anything he or she can buy or do. Only Jesus can get us there. The challenge he gave to the rich man is the same challenge he gives to us today: 'Follow me'.

Ideas for music

Choose hymns and songs which focus on the expected coming of Jesus and are about the simple, uncluttered life-style that God wants us to have in the meantime.

'How lovely on the mountains (Our God reigns)'
'Make way, make way'
'Blessed be the name of the Lord'
'Jesus, lover of my soul' (It's all about you.)
'What do you give a God who has everything?'
'You can't catch a plane'
'Give thanks with a grateful heart'
'Lord, you are more precious than silver'
'The greatest thing in all my life'
'Lord, the light of your love [Shine, Jesus, shine]'
'O Jesus I have promised'
'Take my life and let it be'

Prayers
Intercessions
Copy a world map onto acetate to display on an overhead projector. As you pray for the wealthy countries of the world, place a coin of a distinctive shape (in the UK, for instance, a twenty pence piece) so that the coin partially hides the

countries which fall into that category. As you pray for poor countries, place a grain of rice over countries to which the prayer might apply. It may be interesting at the end to ask people to note whether the way the symbols are clustered seems significant to them.

O God of all people on earth:
We pray for the rich countries.
Help them to use their wealth wisely;
Guide those who decide how the wealth is shared;
Shake them out of selfishness and greed,
And may their riches not blind them to Jesus' call to follow.
O God of all people on earth:
We pray for the poor countries.
Protect them from famine, disease and catastrophe;
Raise up leaders who will inspire and not corrupt them;
Change the hearts of those who have crippled them with debt,
And may their poverty lead them to seek the generosity of Jesus.
O God of all people on earth,
May rich and poor alike find their life in you.

Responsive prayer
Everything comes from you, Lord.
Everything comes from you.
All that I have is yours, Lord.
All that I have is yours.
Out of my love, I give, Lord.
Out of my love, I give.
Take what I offer you, Lord,
Take what I offer you.
I give all I have to you, Lord.
I give all I have to you.
Gladly I follow you, Lord.
Gladly I follow you.

Responding to God
Invite everyone, with their eyes shut, to clench their fists tightly. Ask them to consider their relationship with Jesus - what does it cost them, what holds them back, what do they argue with him about, what is he asking of them this very week? Say

that while some music plays, there will be an opportunity for them to consider his call to follow him ever closer. When and if they feel ready to dedicate themselves to his service (whether for the first or the thousandth time), they can open their hands as a private sign that they have let go of those things that hold them back and entrusted themselves to him. As the music comes to an end, the leader reads these words by J W van Deventer, which could lead into singing the hymn from which they come:

All to Jesus I surrender,
All to him I freely give.
I will ever love and trust him,
In his presence daily live.
I surrender all, I surrender all.
All to you my blessed Saviour,
I surrender all.

christmas-nativity service

SERVICE THEME
Joy to the world

CHURCH YEAR
Christmas – Nativity service

BIBLE BASE
Matthew 2:1–12; Luke 2:1–20

ALL-AGE SERVICE SUMMARY
This service is designed as a special event not only for regular churchgoers, but also for others in the neighbourhood with less or no commitment to regular worship and who might be invited to attend. During the service, a large mock Bible is opened and used as a backdrop for a stable scene which is gradually built. Bible readings from Luke 2 and Matthew 2 can be chosen and placed throughout the service as desired.

THIS WEEK'S RESOURCES
A fully scripted service is provided. Some preparation for children's groups is assumed (see the section: 'Preparation'), but they will not need to rehearse or be in costume. The preparation could equally well be done by adults or young people if it is difficult to arrange for children to do it.

Preparation

Beforehand the following items need to be prepared:
1 The 'Bible': two pieces of hardboard, perhaps each one 1 metre x 80cm hinged together. On the front the words 'The Bible' are written beautifully. When opened, the inside of the book will create a free-standing backdrop for the stable scene.
2 Stars: These should be made for (or preferably by) the youngest children and should be waiting on a table at the side of the room with *Blu-tack* or similar adhesive already attached to them.
3 Straw and a model feeding trough: this also needs to be placed on the table.
4 Sheep and angels: These can be made for or by children aged approximately five to seven years.
5 Figures of Mary, Joseph, the newly-born Jesus, a group of shepherds and a group of wise men: made by junior-age children.
6 Prayers: read (or written and read) by young people.

Script 1

The waiting is nearly over. The homes are being decorated. The gifts are being wrapped. All across the world, people are looking forward to the big day. But, for a short while, we are going to do something different. We are going to look back to the night, hundreds of years ago, when there were no decorations, no wrapping paper, not even the warmth of a home - the night when Jesus Christ was born: the very greatest gift, the very first Christmas. So I invite you, faithful people of *(your town)*, come with us in your imagination. Come to Bethlehem to behold him, Jesus Christ the Lord.

Carol
'O come all you (ye) faithful'

Script 2

Long ago God's people, the Jews, were also waiting. They were waiting for a gift God had promised them - a very special person who would help them in their difficulties and save them from their enemies. They called that person 'the Christ'. But the Jews did not know how long they would have to wait. Already it was many years since God had promised them this wonderful leader and some had given up hope. But many continued to wait for the gift, and they searched the parts of the Bible that they possessed to find out all they could about him. Those who studied hard had worked out that the Christ was going to be born in Bethlehem, a suburb of Jerusalem where David had been king many years before. I suppose they imagined this great man would be born in a palace or a temple, so it is no surprise that hardly anyone paid attention to a dingy cave behind a hotel, in which cows and goats were kept. But *we* know that once, in Bethlehem, (David's city) there stood a lowly cattle shed...

Carol
'Once in Royal David's city'
While this is sung some children open up the hardboard Bible and prop it open, creating a V-shaped backdrop on which a simple outline of a cave has been painted. They take straw from the table, scatter it in front of the backdrop, then put the trough in it (see illustration on p15).

Script 3

Bethlehem was a confusing place to be that night. You see, the Emperor Augustus had conquered so many nations that he had no idea how many people he ruled over. So he decided to take a census and count them all. Everyone, no matter where they lived, had to return to where they had been born. So Bethlehem was full of strangers trying to get a bed for the night. There were to be no excuses. Even if you were old or ill, you had to go. Augustus would not even make exceptions if you were pregnant - not even if your baby was due to be born any day!

Now that is particularly important for two people in the true story we have to tell, for Mary was expecting her baby very soon indeed. She must have been anxious because she knew already that her son was going to be no ordinary baby. An angel had visited her and told her that her baby would be the very person the Jews were waiting for: she was to be the mother of the Christ.

Fortunately, she was not travelling alone. With her was Joseph, who also knew exactly who her unborn baby was, for an angel had visited him too. He was a faithful friend to her and had promised to marry her.

I imagine they travelled slowly so as not to harm the baby. The result was that, by the time they arrived, the hotel had no rooms left and the only shelter they could find was the stable we have sung about. And yes, that is where the Christ, the long-expected hero of the Jews, was born. And they named him Jesus - that's why he is sometimes called Jesus Christ. Like any other baby born in poverty, he was wrapped in rags and, because there was nowhere else to put him, Mary placed the holy infant in the animals' feeding trough, a cattle stall.

Carol
'Infant holy, infant lowly'
Children place the figures of Jesus, Mary and Joseph around the trough.

Script 4

Not very Christmassy, is it? Not very jolly! An unmarried mother, her fiancé and the long-expected Christ stuck in a smelly stable, waiting for the morning. But God plans things in quite different ways from us, and he knew something that no one in Bethlehem knew that night. God himself was the Father of that child, and his Son Jesus whose heart was beginning to pump, pump the blood around his tiny veins, was his gift to the world - for that baby grew into the child, who grew into the teenager, who grew into the man who did everything it took for humans to live as forgiven people, restored as God's friends. So let us imagine Mary, Joseph and Jesus as silently, silently the wondrous gift is given and, as Bethlehem sleeps, deep and dreamless, we will watch the silent stars go by.

Carol
'O little town of Bethlehem'
The youngest children collect their stars from the table, accompanied by adults, and attach them all around the top and edges of the Nativity scene. A particularly large star could be placed in the centre.

nativity service

Script 5

If you knew that the Christ had been born, who would you tell? The prime minister? The king or queen? Well, God chose to tell some shepherds on a hill outside Bethlehem. Perhaps they were the only people awake at dead of night, as they guarded their sheep against robbers and wild animals. Suddenly, to their amazement, they saw the sky full of angels telling them that the Christ they had been waiting for was born. The angels told them where to find the baby and how they would know he was the right one. 'Glory to God in the highest,' sang the angels, 'and peace to all people on earth, for God is pleased with them!' The shepherds rushed into town and searched out the place where Jesus and his family were resting. And all the people they told were amazed at what the shepherds had seen while they watched their flocks by night.

Carol

'While shepherds watched their flocks by night'
The children who made the shepherds and sheep collect them and take them to the centre, arranging them in and around the scene. The angels should also be moved to an appropriate position.

Script 6

And so Jesus was born - the Christ for whom the Jews had waited, born into a Jewish family, visited and talked of by Jewish shepherds. But God had bigger plans for this world than the Jews even dared imagine. His plan was not just to bring back the Jewish people to be his friends - his plan was to bring people from the entire world, pole to pole, into his family. And while Jesus was crying and feeding and sleeping in a stable in Bethlehem, his birth was having an impact on people hundreds of miles away too. Way in the East, a group of scholarly men, who studied the great mysteries of the world, became convinced that the time was right for the Christ to be born. They left their homes and set out on a journey to find him. They knew where to go because God made sure that a particular star was in place as a sign. They went first to Jerusalem and then followed the star to Bethlehem where, overflowing with joy, they realised that God had led them to the very place where Christ was living.

This was probably some time later, and Jesus may have been a toddler when they arrived, but let's place them in the stable too, so that we can see them offer gifts to the young Jesus: precious gold, sweet-smelling frankincense, and a spice called myrrh. But most of all, let's join them in worshipping Jesus, for they were the very first people who were not Jews to sing praise with one accord to the heavenly Lord, and we in this room are the most recent.

Carol

'The first Nowell'
Children collect the figures of the wise men and place them on the edge of the Nativity scene.

Prayers

These prayers could be led by a group of young people, the words divided up amongst them. Some may prefer them to devise and lead their own prayers to offer at this point.

A: Lord Jesus, you were born many miles from your home;
B: We pray for those who are homeless this Christmas;
C: Give them your peace, Lord,
All: And show us how to help them.
A: Lord Jesus, you were born shut out of an inn which was full of people;
B: We pray for those who will be lonely this week, or sad because they are trying to cope without someone they love;
C: Give them your peace, Lord,
All: And show us how to help them.
A: Lord Jesus, you were born in poverty;
B: We pray for those who have felt obliged to spend too much this Christmas and face a worrying future;
C: Give them your peace, Lord,
All: And show us how to help them.
A: Lord Jesus, you were born in the night and only a handful of people recognised who you were;
B: We pray for the millions of people who have never heard that Jesus Christ was born on earth and have never received your gift to the world;
C: Give them your peace, Lord,
All: And show us how to help them. Amen.

Script 7

So now our Nativity scene is complete. Try not to forget it in the whirlwind of the next few days. Let it remind you of the great gift God has given to the world - Jesus Christ, the one through whom friendship can be enjoyed, forgiveness can be assured, and a true peace can be found. May we wish you a very happy Christmas, and may the Lord bless you and keep you, may the Lord make his face shine upon you, may the Lord turn his face toward you and give you his peace, this week and for evermore.

Carol

'It came upon a midnight clear'

christmas-nativity service

SERVICE THEME
Surprises at Christmas

CHURCH YEAR
Christmas – Nativity service

BIBLE BASE
Matthew 2:1-12; Luke 2:1-20

ALL-AGE SERVICE SUMMARY
The Christmas story is told in a straightforward way, focusing on some of the unlikely, surprising aspects of the events surrounding the birth of Jesus.

THIS WEEK'S RESOURCES
This is a Nativity from scratch! It needs little preparation and no rehearsals, but there is scope for plenty of participation by those who want to get involved. A full script is provided and prayers and Bible readings can be added as you wish.

Preparation

To outside observers, it will appear that the Christmas story has been told using the people and objects that happen to be in the church building on the day. This is basically true. Some adults and children will come to the service expecting to go unnoticed and find themselves the 'stars' - perhaps even people who have not been to church for a long time will feel that they have been welcomed as insiders. Others will find that they have brought with them something that becomes a vital prop in the telling of the story. (In fact the spontaneity needs to be helped on its way by you planting a few of the items in the room in advance. You may not need them, but you will be grateful for the security of knowing they are there.) You will need:

1 Thirteen adults and children to play the Nativity roles (these genuinely do not need to be informed in advance and they will not need to put on costumes).
2 Thirteen file cards bearing the words: Mary, Joseph, star, angel (4 of these), shepherd (3), wise man (3).
3 A blue scarf, cardigan or sweater.
4 A walking stick (trust that someone will have one of these and, if no one does, there will be fun to be had in improvising with whatever is in the room - perhaps a window opener or an umbrella).

5 A chair.
6 Something to represent a manger. (It will be interesting to see what is offered - perhaps a baby seat - but if no one in the congregation can think of anything spontaneously, have a box of church lost property or books sitting at the back ready to be emptied and used.)
7 A toy sheep. (Plant this - it is just possible that a child will bring one, but avoid disappointment by making sure.)
8 A star, tinsel and wrapped presents. (To be sure of having these, put a decorated Christmas tree somewhere near the front of the building, making sure that the star on the top, the gifts underneath and the tinsel are easily detachable.)
9 A doll. (There is bound to be a child who will part briefly with her doll for the scene - if there isn't, using a real baby will add a lively dynamic!)
10 All sorts of things that glitter.
11 Most importantly, you need a really good narrator who will need to be asked in advance. A child or group of children honestly will not do - it has to be someone with the confidence to take control of what is going on, even if it is not happening quite as planned.

Script 1

May I give you a warm welcome and wish you a very happy Christmas! Today we have come together to hear in words and carols the timeless and true story of Jesus Christ, born on the first Christmas Day - God come to live among us.

But where are the actors? Where is the scenery? Where are the props? Well, they are all here in the room with us - they just don't know it yet! In a moment, I am going to come into the congregation and find Mary, Joseph, and all the other characters we need to tell the story. Some will be grown-ups and some will be younger. I'm going to see who catches my eye during this carol, so if you really don't want to take part, keep your head down in the hymn book as we sing 'Once in royal David's city'!

Carol
'Once in royal David's city'
While the congregation is singing, go among them locating people who look as though they would enjoy being part of the production. Give the ones you choose a card which tells them what part they are playing. As you do so, individually reassure them of four things - you will not embarrass them; they will not need to dress up; there are no words to say; you will tell them precisely what to do and when to do it.

christmas-nativity service

Script 2

Our story starts not in David's city, Bethlehem, but in Nazareth many miles to the north. A woman named Mary was pregnant. She must have been anxious because she knew her son would be no ordinary baby. An angel had visited her and told her that the baby she was expecting would be the Messiah, the great Saviour for whom the Jews had been waiting for very many years. It was a census that took her on the long journey to Bethlehem with Joseph.

When they arrived in Bethlehem, there was no room left at the hotel. The only shelter they could find was in a stable. So it was there, in the little town of Bethlehem, that the anxious and exhausted couple waited under the stars for Mary's time to come.

As we sing 'O little town of Bethlehem', would those who have 'Mary' and 'Joseph' written on their cards please join me to begin to form our Christmas tableau.

Carol
'O little town of Bethlehem'
While the congregation sing, Mary and Joseph come to the front. Arrange them so that Mary is sitting on a chair, with Joseph standing beside her.

Script 3

So it was there that their son Jesus was born. And because there was nowhere else to put him, Mary placed the holy child in the animal's feeding trough, a manger.

At this point, I need a little help from the rest of the congregation. There are three things which we need to add to the picture we are forming. Ancient paintings always show Mary dressed in blue, because blue was the most costly paint available to them. If anyone came to church wearing a blue scarf, jacket or coat, please could they spare it to put around Mary's shoulders? And Joseph needs a crook because he is going to be standing here for a long time - a walking stick would be perfect, but perhaps you could think of something better? The third thing needs a little imagination! We need something to stand in for a manger. Any ideas? What about a baby seat, or an empty box? Have a look around the church and see what you can find. If you can provide any of those things, please bring them to the front while we sing 'Infant holy'.

Carol
'Infant holy, infant lowly'
Mary's wrap, Joseph's stick and the manger are added to the scene.

Script 4

Some of the residents of Bethlehem were about to have a great surprise, because God chose them to be the very first to know that Jesus Christ, the Messiah, their Saviour, had been born. It was such a joyous message that it could only be given with a lavish spectacle and sensational music. On a hillside outside the town God filled the sky with angels singing, 'Praise be to the Lord in heaven and peace to all who live on earth. Don't be afraid,' they went on, 'for this is good news which will bring world-wide happiness.'

So let's add the angels to the picture. If you have a card which shows that you are an angel, please come and join me. You will need a halo to show who you are, so if anyone has brought tinsel with them to church, now is the time to use it. There is plenty on the Christmas tree, so you could take some from there and make a halo with it. While you are doing that, we are all going to sing 'Hark the herald angels sing'.

Carol
'Hark the herald angels sing'
Show the angels where to stand.

Script 5

The angels sang their song to a group of shepherds who were out in the fields guarding their sheep from thieves and wild animals. When they heard what the angels had to say, they ran from door to door in Bethlehem. Where was the newborn baby? They found him at last in the stable, and told Mary and Joseph what the angels had said about Jesus. Everyone was astonished by the message, but Mary never forgot these things. She kept thinking about them year in, year out, as the child grew to be a man. And what a man - Jesus the Messiah, God walking and talking among us.

While we sing 'See amid the winter's snow', let's add the shepherds to our scene.

Carol
'See amid the winter's snow'
Place the shepherds in the tableau, some sitting, some standing.

Script 6

All we need now is a sheep! *(It would add great merriment if this was a pre-arranged sign for the toy sheep to come curving through the air and land in your arms.)*

Many miles away in the East, a group of scholarly men had become convinced through their studies that this was the right time for the Messiah to be born. They left their homes to make the long journey to seek him out. They knew where to go because God made sure that a particular star was in place as a sign for them. They followed the star to Bethlehem, where Jesus was living. They went into the house, worshipped Jesus and gave him their gifts of gold, frankincense and myrrh.

Our wise men will need to find gifts to bring with them to the display. I'm sure someone in the church has something suitable that they would be prepared to lend for a little while. If not, have a look under the Christmas tree. The person who has a card saying 'star' will need to find a star, perhaps on the tree. Meanwhile, let's enjoy singing 'We three kings of Orient are'.

Carol
'We three kings of Orient are'
Arrange the wise men, kneeling before the manger, and place the person holding the star behind the others.

Script 7

And that was how it was that the Saviour of the world was born - worshipped by shepherds, worshipped by angels and now worshipped by us. He is the one who takes our wrongdoing and guilt away and makes us friends with God again.

There is one more thing that we need to add to our nativity scene, and that is the baby Jesus. Has anyone brought a doll to church with them today, which I could borrow to make the scene complete? *(Go out into the congregation as you say this, and find a child who has brought their doll. Keep talking as you go. Take the doll and lay it in whatever you are using as a manger.)*

Thank you very much for sparing your doll to make the tableau perfect. And now, if you are very young, there is a chance for you to come to the front and sit around the scene we have made so that you can have a better look. You are going to represent the stars in the night sky, so bring with you anything that glitters - ask the grown-ups you are sitting with if you can borrow their keys, their coins, their diamond tiaras, anything that will sparkle in the light. We can all wave them in the air as we sing 'Away in a manger'.

Carol
'Away in a manger'
As the children converge during this, show them where to sit and how to wave in time with the music. Give tinsel to any children who are empty-handed. If it is possible, it would be moving for something full of wonder to happen to the lighting at this point - perhaps candles could be brought to surround the scene, or if it is dark outside the lights could be dimmed so that just one illuminates the picture, or (technically difficult, but a talking point well into the new year) a mirror ball could send lights shimmering around the room.

Carol
'O come all you (ye) faithful'
As this is sung, tell those who are at the front to return to their places. This can be done individually which gives you a chance to thank them in person for what they have contributed as their act of worship.

christmas-
nativity service

Introduction

Leader: Welcome to this joyful service. May I wish you a very happy Christmas. Today we are going to make a journey, in our imaginations, back through the years to a cold night in Bethlehem. May God speed us on our journey, and may what we find there fill us with hope. This Christmas-time, let us join with millions around the world singing praise to the Lord Jesus, the Saviour of the world. Let our carols add to the music of the countless billions of the heavenly host, for we are joining our song with the song the angels sing.

Carol
'Angels from the realms of glory'

Script 1

A soldier enters. As he gets to a central position, he is taken by surprise by a disembodied voice. He looks up, as if he does not know where it comes from, before replying.
Voice: Where are you going?
Soldier: I'm going to Bethlehem.
Voice: Why are you going there?
Soldier: I'm under orders from the Emperor Augustus. He has conquered so many countries that he has decided to take a census to count how many people he rules. It's fallen to us in the army to do the counting. Not my kind of thing at all – I'm more used to fighting than counting. *(He counts on his fingers.)* Eye, eye-eye, eye-eye-eye, eye-vee, vee. I wish I'd listened more in maths class.
Voice: What are you expecting to find there?
Soldier: Chaos, I expect! Everyone has to return to the place they were born in order to register. It feels like the whole of Israel is on the move. I'm glad I've got the barracks to sleep in tonight. I'd hate to be fighting for a place in one of the hotels.
Voice: Are you travelling with joy in your heart?
Soldier: Joy? Don't know about that! When the emperor says 'Go', you go. Even if you're old, even if you're sick, even if you're pregnant like the poor soul I've just passed on the road. What a way to be born, eh! Heaven knows what will become of that

little scrap!
Voice: Perhaps heaven has been planning this for longer than you think!
Soldier: Whatever do you mean by that?
Voice: God speed you on your journey. May what you find there fill you with hope.
Soldier: Thank you.
Voice: And listen, for you may hear the angels sing.
Soldier: I will. *(He goes.)*

Carol
'O little town of Bethlehem'

Script 2

Two midwives enter, in the same way as the soldier. The words that follow are split between the two of them (although it would be possible to have only one).
Voice: Where are you going?
Midwife 1: We're going to Bethlehem.
Voice: Why are you going there?
Midwife 2: We are midwives. We have heard that one of the women in Bethlehem needs our help. She is about to give birth to her first baby, so we need to get there straightaway.
Voice: What are you expecting to find there?
Midwife 1: We don't know what to expect. Someone came rushing to find us and said that she heard a woman crying for help in a cattle barn. What a dreadful place for the

baby to be born. Bethlehem is full to bursting with people today - perhaps there was no room left in the inn.

Voice: Are you travelling with joy in your hearts?

Midwife 2: It is always a joy to see a baby brought into the world. We worship God, who is the great life-giver. But how terrible that the child has to be born in such poverty.

Midwife 1: How can people be so cruel that they don't make room for someone so precious? We are determined to deliver the child safely.

Voice: Perhaps it will be the child who delivers you!

Midwives: Whatever do you mean by that?

Voice: God speed your journey. May what you find there fill you with hope.

Midwife 1: Thank you.

Voice: And listen, for you may hear the angels sing.

Midwife 2: We will. *(They go.)*

Carol
'Once in royal David's city'

Bible reading
Luke 2:1-7

Script 3

A shepherd enters, as before. (Again, this could be rearranged for more than one shepherd.)

Voice: Where are you going?

Shepherd: I'm going to Bethlehem.

Voice: Why are you going there?

Shepherd: Well, I can barely believe it, but I think an angel has sent me there. I was out on the hillside doing my job, making sure the sheep were safe from harm. All of a sudden the sky was filled with lights and voices. They told me to go to Bethlehem straightaway, so I abandoned the sheep and ran.

Voice: What are you expecting to find there?

Shepherd: Well, the angel says that a baby has been born. He's lying in an animal's manger. Not an ordinary baby - it's the Messiah, God's own Saviour! We have been waiting for him for so long that I can barely take it in.

Voice: Are you travelling with joy in your heart?

Shepherd: Joy! I'm terrified! I feel that I've been in the presence of God himself. And I shall be in terrible trouble from the boss for leaving the sheep. But I can't resist going to see what's happening. I shall just have to keep it a secret that I'm doing this.

Voice: But you are about to enter the presence of God all over again - God born on earth! And you won't be able to resist telling everyone you meet, so it won't be a secret for long.

Shepherd: Whatever do you mean by that?

Voice: God speed you on your journey. May what you find there fill you with hope.

Shepherd: Thank you.

Voice: And listen, for you may hear the angels sing.

Shepherd: I will. *(He goes.)*

Carol
'While shepherds watch their flocks'

Bible reading
Luke 2:8-20

Script 4

A wise man (or more than one) enters.

Voice: Where are you going?

Wise man: I'm going to Bethlehem.

Voice: Why are you going there?

Wise man: My friends and I have come a great distance from Far Eastern lands. We have read the great books of the Jews and we have studied the great stars of the sky. We have followed a star thus far, and we will follow it until we have found the one we have come to worship.

Voice: What are you expecting to find there?

Wise man: A king! The king of the Jews. We have looked for him in the magnificent palace of Jerusalem, but he was not there - just the great ruler Herod, afraid that his power is under threat. He has directed us to Bethlehem to find the child born to be king. Herod asks that we return and report to him, so that he too may worship.

Voice: Are you travelling with joy in your heart?

Wise man: With joy in our hearts and gifts in our luggage - gold, frankincense, myrrh. But we are fearful too. We will not return to Herod, for we believe he means to harm the child. We are wise men - we know who to worship and who to obey.

Voice: Wise men - and women and children - will always obey and worship this king!

Wise man: Whatever do you mean by that?

Voice: God speed you on your journey. May what you find there fill you with hope.

Wise man: Thank you.

Voice: And listen, for you may hear the angels sing.

Wise man: I will. *(He goes.)*

Bible reading
Matthew 2:1-12

Carol
'As with gladness men of old'

Script 5

A teenager, in modern dress with a rucksack on his or her back, enters.

Voice: Where are you going?

Teenager: I'm going to Bethlehem.

Voice: Why are you going there?

Teenager: I'm exploring the world. If you can't do that when you're young, when can you do it? I've always wanted to go to Israel.

Voice: What are you expecting to find there?

Teenager: Well, many hundreds of years ago Jesus was born there. I'm

christmas-nativity servic

going to see the place where he was born and the towns in which he lived. You see, I'm a Christian and I try to live my life in the way he wants me to. The more I understand him, the more I want to worship him.

Voice: Are you travelling with joy in your heart?

Teenager: I've heard that it's a sad and dangerous place now, so I'm anxious. But the world was a sad and dangerous place when he lived too - that's why he needed to come.

Voice: Perhaps you will find that Jesus is more alive in you than in any old building you see!

Teenager: Whatever do you mean by that?

Voice: God speed you on your journey. May what you find there fill you with hope.

Teenager: Thank you.

Voice: And listen, for you may hear the angels sing.

Teenager: I will. *(He/she goes.)*

Carol
'O come all you (ye) faithful'

Script 6

Several children enter. They could be from a range of ages, with the words divided between the older ones.

Voice: Where are you going?

Children: We're going to Bethlehem.

Voice: Why are you going?

Children: To find the baby Jesus.

Voice: But it was many, many years ago that he was born.

Children: We know that, silly! We're pretending!

Voice: Are you travelling with joy in your heart?

Children: Of course we are. It's Christmas! There's presents to open and food to enjoy!

Voice: If you do find Jesus this Christmas, you will realise that there is much more than presents and food to enjoy - there is peace with God, there is forgiveness of all that is wrong, and there is true wonder!

Children: Whatever do you mean by that?

Voice: God speed you on your journey. May what you find fill you with hope.

Children: Thank you.

Voice: And listen, for you may hear the angels sing.

Children: We will. *(They go.)*

Climax

Leader: Well, what a lot of people heading for Bethlehem. I wonder what they will find there! Let's watch and find out. And listen as well, because we too may hear the angels sing.

[Beautiful music begins (either performed live or played through a sound system). Two adults or children dressed as Mary and Joseph take their place at the front of the room. They are carrying a baby (either real or a doll). All those who have taken part so far gather round them in a carefully arranged tableau.

The lights dim to candle-light. There is wonder in the air. Hold this for a little while.]

Leader: And so let us pray. We join the hosts of angels praising God and saying, 'Glory to God in the highest, and on earth peace to all on whom his favour rests.' Lord Jesus Christ, born in a stable, may you be born in our lives; king of all ages, may we come to worship you as our king; Prince of Peace, may you bring peace in our homes, peace between the peoples of the world, and peace between humankind and the Almighty God. Amen.

And may the blessing of God the Father, the Son and the Holy Spirit rest upon us and all those we love this Christmas, for hark the herald angels indeed do sing: 'Glory to the newborn king!'

Carol
'Hark, the herald angels sing'

christmas day
christmas day

OUTLINE 7

SERVICE THEME
Great expectations

CHURCH YEAR
Christmas Day

BIBLE BASE
Luke 2:1–7

ALL-AGE SERVICE SUMMARY
The unexpected nature of Christ's birth is the theme of this service. It also explores the reason for his coming to earth and the expectations that God has for us as the followers of Jesus.

THIS WEEK'S RESOURCES
For this service, there is plenty of activity to involve excitable children, so be sure not to omit these sections! If you are using the praise suggestion in the section 'Colourful praise', you will need to prime people on the previous Sunday.

Setting the scene

Prepare a parcel which will be progressively unwrapped. In the centre, place something for the congregation to share - a large jar of sweets would be suitable. Wrap this up in plain brown paper. The next layer will be birthday gift paper and the outer wrapper 'new baby' gift paper of the kind that is used for a present marking a new birth.

Produce the parcel and take off one layer at a time with the help of some of the youngest children and talk briefly about the significance of each type of paper. The 'baby' paper reminds us that Mary had been promised a son; the birthday paper reminds us of the meaning of Christmas day - the birth of our Saviour Jesus Christ; the brown paper recalls that the birth was not splendid or colourful or luxurious, but cold, painful and in great poverty. That is the fearful reality of how God came among us on earth and yet it is a cause of great celebration - God has come among us as a baby. Share out the sweets!

Bible reading

Luke 2:1–7
The reading could be read slowly with a small group of children and adults miming. (It is not necessary for any of the actors to wear costume.) Two men representing the Emperor Augustus and Quirinius enter after the reading has been announced and turn their backs on

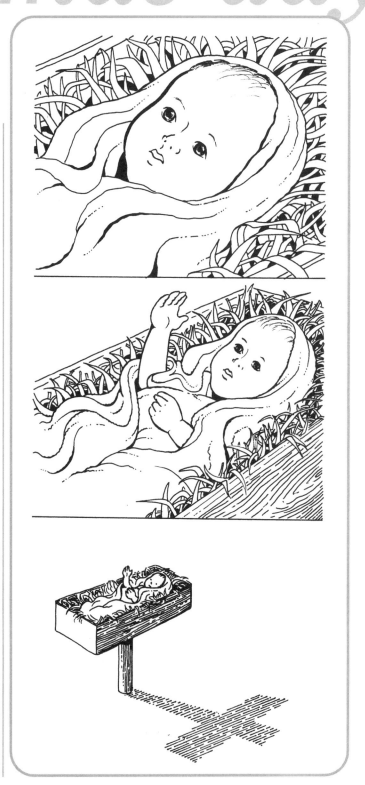

christmas day

the congregation. As their names are mentioned, they turn and stand in imposing stance, Augustus pointing as though giving an order. Joseph and Mary enter from the back of the room as Joseph is mentioned, and walk slowly to the front, watched by Augustus and Quirinius. The reader should pause at the end of verse 5 until Mary and Joseph have reached the front and sit or stand huddled together, looking weary and dejected. During verse 7, Mary mimes picking up a tiny baby and passing it to Joseph who holds him out to the congregation. As he does this, Augustus and Quirinius look at one another, alarmed, and turn away, stooping as though defeated. At the end of the reading all freeze for several seconds.

Bible teaching for all ages

Show three Christmas presents that you have received - one that you were expecting, one that is a complete surprise, and one that you particularly need. (Obviously, this could be faked.) Ask members of the congregation for examples of presents they have opened in the same three categories. Use, for the visual aids for the talk, the illustrations on page 23 enlarged or photocopied onto acetate to use on an overhead projector.

Just what I expected!

Show the picture of a close-up of a baby's face. This is a newly-born Jesus. For hundreds of years the Jews had been expecting the birth of a great leader who would help them in their difficulties and set them free from their enemies. They called him 'the Christ'. So God's present to the earth - Jesus - was 'just what they expected'.

Not what I expected!

The next picture pulls back slightly to reveal that the baby is in a manger. What's this? Hardly the place you would expect a great

leader to be born! The great surprise of Christmas is that God came to earth not in splendour, but in poverty. That's why so few people recognised that he was the long-expected Christ. But the shepherds did, and they went away 'glorifying and praising God'.

Just what I needed!

Pulling back, the manger can be seen to throw the shadow of the cross. Being born as a human was the only way God could bring about the forgiveness we need to reunite us with him. Because of the birth, death and resurrection of Jesus, we can share friendship with him now and forever. There is nothing we need more! Happy Christmas!

Ideas for music

Choose well-known carols and other songs which focus on the birth of Jesus.
Examples:
'Come and join the celebration'
'O come all you (ye) faithful'
'Once in royal David's city'
'See amid the winter's snow'
'See him lying on a bed of straw'

Prayers

Colourful praise

As the congregation arrives, have people ready at the door to collect the used gift-wrapping paper that they were asked to bring during the preceding week. At some point during the service (perhaps during the singing of carols), invite children below a certain age to go to a space in the room where a large piece of lining paper, paste, and a couple of adult supervisors are waiting. They should use the wrapping paper (torn meanwhile into postcard-sized pieces) to create a large banner which says 'Welcome Jesus'. The letters that make up the words should be pencilled in advance, and the children encouraged to paste their coloured paper inside the lines. When it is finished, bring it to the front of the room and thank the

children for their colourful contribution to the service - an act of praise to Jesus. Say a short prayer which helps people ask Jesus to be welcome in their homes this Christmas.

Loving and needing Jesus

Holy child of Bethlehem, you became a stranger so that we might belong. Lord Jesus...
We love you and we need you.
You were forced on a journey so that we might be set free. Lord Jesus...
We love you and we need you.
You were born in a homeless family so that we might be at home. Lord Jesus...
We love you and we need you.
You were born a child in a manger so that we might reign in glory with you. Lord Jesus...
We love you and we need you.
Come to us anew and fulfil our expectations. Lord Jesus...
We love you and we need you.

Intercessions

Pray for those who are lonely today, for those who have been bereaved during the year, for those in debt, for those with no home and for those whose tempers could be frayed at this stressful time. Thank God for the work of the Samaritans and other 'listening ear' organisations and those providing shelter for the homeless. Ask God to give their volunteer workers skill, fulfilment and resistance to tiredness.

Dedication

Lord Jesus, we expected splendour, but you came in poverty. Now you expect us to serve the poor generously.
We expected a king, but you came as a baby. Now you expect us to protect the weak and defenceless.
We expected beauty, but you came in squalor. Now you expect us to enrich the world of those who find it a harsh place.
With deep thanks and humble praise, we offer ourselves in your service. Amen.

christmas
christmas day

OUTLINE 8

SERVICE THEME
Jesus, the Light of the world

CHURCH YEAR
Christmas Day

BIBLE BASE
John 1:1-14

ALL-AGE SERVICE SUMMARY
The service explores the meaning of the description of Jesus as the Light of the world. There are opportunities for all ages to participate without the need for any rehearsal.

THIS WEEK'S RESOURCES
It is assumed that the whole family of the church will worship together on this day. Arrange and add to the resources to suit your own congregation.

A procession of light

The service could begin with a procession of children and adults with lanterns, candles, torches and so on. They should be placed at the front of the room as a visual symbol of worship of the 'Light of the world'.

Setting the scene

Invite the congregation to turn to each other, children and adults in clusters of two or three. Show the picture below, which should either be transferred to an overhead projector acetate or photocopied so that every cluster has one between

them. Ask them to identify as many different kinds of light as possible in the picture. After a minute or so of discussion, regain the congregation's attention and ask some of them to call out what they have found. In each case, highlight the specific value of that light (for example, headlights show us the way, traffic lights provide control, etc).

Bible reading
John 1:1-14

Choose three readers with very different voices - perhaps a man, a woman and an older child. Ask one

to read all the phrases and verses containing the word 'Word', another to read those containing the word 'light' and the third to read those which contain the word 'God' or 'Father' and all other verses. When 'Word' and 'light' and/or 'God' appear in the same verse, the two readers should read together.

Bible teaching for all ages

In preparation, cut from paper the following letters: W, O, R, D (x2), G. Each letter should be about 5 cms high. Tape them to the inside of a

large lampshade with the letters 'WORD' reading horizontally and 'GOD' vertically, the two words intersecting at the letter O. Set the lamp up connected to the electricity supply (with the lampshade in place), ready to be switched on at the end of the talk.

You will also need four sealed envelopes in which are written four Bible verses in a text that is clear enough for older children to read (but not in capital letters). Introduce the idea of secret signs and symbols in John 1:1-14. The 'Word' is God. 'God' is revealed in Jesus. 'Jesus' is described as 'light' - he said 'I am the light of the world'. (John 8:12). We have already seen that light controls, illuminates, warns, etc. Jesus in fact does all three things. Specifically he is:

The light of knowledge

Invite a child to open the first envelope and read out 2 Corinthians 4:6. Jesus shows us everything we need to know about God. He said, 'If you've seen me, you've seen the Father'. Where Jesus is loving, so is God; where Jesus is powerful, so is God, and so on.

The light of judgement

Invite another child to open envelope two and read John 3:19. Jesus shows us everything we need to know about ourselves. Tell the story of a boy hiding in the cupboard under the stairs, playing at hide and seek. He only realises what the cupboard is really like when he switches on his torch and sees cobwebs, dust and dirt. Jesus shows up the darkness and wrong in our lives. Jesus was announced as the Saviour - the one who comes to change people's lives and make them light.

The light of life

The third child reads John 9:5. Give a brief example of how plants need light for life. Remind the congregation of how Jesus brought

'light' to those who met him - sometimes literally by helping blind people see; often by helping them see wonderful things about life that they had not seen before.

The light of direction

The fourth envelope contains Psalm 119:105. God's word is a lamp to our feet and a light to our path. (This is the point at which to switch the lamp on and reveal the words.) If we follow Jesus, as revealed through the Bible, we are following the person who knows the right way to go. There is no better decision that you could make this Christmas Day.

Ideas for music

Choose traditional carols and other Christmas songs which mention light, the 'Word' or focus on Jesus as the Light of the world.
Examples:
'Holy child, how still you lie'
'Light has dawned'
'Long ago in Bethlehem'
'O come all you (ye) faithful'
'Shine Jesus shine'
'Christians awake, salute the happy morn'
'Unto us a child is born'
'There's a place where the streets shine'
'We'll walk the land'

Danced carol

While the congregation sings 'O come all ye faithful', a group performs the following dance steps, which are reproduced courtesy of Mary Jones (Christian Dance Fellowship of Australia). The dancers process across the space available using the tripudium step (explained below) during the verse, and during the refrains perform the movements indicated below. (Incidentally, the tripudium step was used in church processions during the Middle Ages. It symbolises the Christian walk, expressing the fact that even though we sin and fall back, we do make progress as we are forgiven and start forwards again.)

During the verses: *Tripudium step (walk counter-clockwise, slowly in a circle - right foot, left foot, right foot, then rock back on left foot - and continue the pattern, forming a circle as the verse comes to a close).*
During the refrain: O come let us adore him, *(take one step towards the centre of the circle, then reach hands out in invitation to those around the circle);*
O come let us adore him, *(kneel in worship, imagining the manger in the centre of the circle and reaching out with hands cupped towards it in adoration gesture);*
O come let us adore him, *(stand and lift arms in gesture of worship to the risen Lord);*
Christ the Lord, *(step back while bowing).*

Prayers

Responsive prayer

Either an individual, a group or the whole congregation echoes the words in italics after the leader. The prayer is by Pat Baker, from *On the Move* magazine, used by permission of United Education, PO Box 1245, Collingwood 3066, Australia:

Where the world is in darkness, send light, *(send light),*
Where there is conflict, bring peace, *(bring peace),*
Where people are hurting, send healing, *(send healing),*
Where there is brokenness, make whole, *(make whole),*
In the emptiness, there is Christ, *(there is Christ).*

Where the world is in darkness, send light, *(send light),*
To sorrowing people send joy, *(send joy),*
Where people despair, bring hope, *(bring hope),*
In the midst of death, speak life, *(speak life),*
In the emptiness, there is Christ, *(there is Christ).*

Where the world is in darkness, send

light, *(send light),*
Where anger rages, bring justice, *(bring justice),*
In the midst of clamour, send silence, *(send silence),*
Where hatred rules, bring love, *(bring love),*
In the emptiness, there is Christ, *(there is Christ).*

Where the world is in darkness, *(send light),*
Where there is blindness, give sight, *(give sight),*
Where storm clouds gather, make rainbows, *(make rainbows),*
In the bitterness of tears, bring laughter, *(bring laughter),*
In the emptiness, there is Christ, *(there is Christ).*

Where the world is in darkness, send light, *(send light),*
Where there is division, bring community, *(bring community),*
In misunderstanding, give patience, *(give patience),*
Where there is blame, send forgiveness, *(send forgiveness),*
In the emptiness, there is Christ, *(there is Christ).*

The biggest surprise of all

I'm so excited, Jesus
Christmas is such a great time - full of gifts and surprises.
But you were the biggest surprise of all
because no one thought you'd come as a tiny baby,
and born in a poor place like a stable.
You were the best gift of all, too,
a gift from God to bring us life forever.
Thank you for being the biggest surprise
And the best gift. Amen.
© Michael Lush

christmas day

christmas day

OUTLINE 9

SERVICE THEME
God becomes a servant

CHURCH YEAR
Christmas Day

BIBLE BASE
Philippians 2:5-11

ALL-AGE SERVICE SUMMARY
Realising afresh that small things can have a large impact and that a tiny baby born in poverty could change the world.

THIS WEEK'S RESOURCES
It is assumed that the whole church family will be worshipping on Christmas Day. Choose from and add to the resources to suit the age balance of those who may be present.

Greeting

At the beginning of the service, teach the congregation these words and actions, based on the song of the angels to the shepherds. It can then be repeated at a point central to the service. (In a church with a tradition of 'passing the peace' that is the ideal moment.) Do it a third time at the close:
Glory to God in the highest (raise hands in the air),
And peace to his people on earth (shake hands with those standing nearby).

Setting the scene

Ask the congregation to form themselves into groups so that half a dozen adults and children are gathered around a pencil and paper. One person from each group should come to the front of the room - neither the youngest nor the oldest, but someone in the middle. Whisper to them the name of an object connected with the Christmas story. They must return to their group and draw it. The person in the group who guesses what it is returns to the front and is told the next object to draw and so on.

The first object to be drawn is a sheep, then a star, a manger, an angel, a shepherd, swaddling clothes (some may need to be told that these are strips of cloth), three wise men.

If there is a large congregation, more helpers will be needed to whisper the objects. Finish the game when about two-thirds of the groups have finished, and congratulate everyone.

Now ask the groups to talk to each other and decide what is the thing that, as a group, they most enjoy about Christmas? They will need to negotiate because only one thing is allowed per group. After a couple of minutes to talk, ask one person in the group to draw what they have settled on. The leader should say a prayer of thanksgiving, so that everyone can focus with gratitude on the particular thing they have drawn.

Bible reading
Philippians 2:5-11
A dramatic way of illustrating the theme of this reading would be to begin with two 'actors' standing together raised from the floor (in a high pulpit or even on a step ladder!). One remains there throughout the reading watching the other. The other, representing Christ, descends lower and lower until crouched on the floor at the end of verse 8. There could be a short pause at this stage. Then, as the first actor opens arms of welcome, the other begins to climb again until both are together again, linking upraised hands.

Bible teaching for all ages

Transfer the photographs on page 29 onto overhead projector acetates, and display them one at a time. They are all pictures of very small things enlarged so that they seem to be bigger than they are. Ask the congregation to work out what they are. (The answers are, clockwise from top left: a light bulb, a floppy disk, a screw, a lemon.)

It may not be possible to use an overhead projector in the church. In this case there are two options. You could photocopy the page onto paper and give one to everyone (or every group) in the church. You will get the best results if you use a photocopier which has a setting specifically for reproducing photographs. The other alternative is to talk about very small things which have a very large impact. For example, a silicon chip is tiny (show one if you can), but it can hold more information than an encyclopedia. A pimple might be minute, but it can be unbearably uncomfortable. The same goes for the pip that grows into an apple tree, or a speck of dust behind a contact lens.

The wonder of the modern age is something extremely small becoming very, very powerful. But there is a wonder of an ancient age as well. It is the wonder of Christmas where something very, very powerful became extremely small. When God chose to reveal himself to

christmas day

humankind, the biggest surprise is that he did not come as a mighty, powerful conqueror; he came as a tiny, helpless baby. The way the Bible describes it is that he emptied himself and became a servant (Philippians 2:7). Why did he do it? Firstly so that he could be an example of how we should live - not as people who want to control each other, but as people who want to serve and help each other.

Secondly, because the only way God could fully help us was to become like us - being born, living life to the full, dying.

Thirdly, so that by triumphing over death, he could allow us to overcome death as well and live in heaven for ever.

That tiny baby is now the almighty and awesomely powerful Jesus Christ, the Lord of heaven and earth (Philippians 2:9-11). There is no better time than Christmas to see him as he really is - the one to worship and obey as Lord.

Ideas for music

Choose songs and carols which speak about the humble birth of Jesus and about the humility with which he served humankind. Examples:

'See amid the winter's snow'
'Come and join the celebration'
'See him lying on a bed of straw'
'Meekness and majesty'
'See, to us a child is born'
'You laid aside your majesty'
'Lord I lift your name on high'
'At the name of Jesus'
'From heaven you came'
'The Servant King'
'Once in royal David's city'

Prayers

Echoes of praise

Lord Jesus, born in Bethlehem,
Lord Jesus, born in Bethlehem,
Welcome to our world
this Christmas;
Welcome to our world this Christmas;
Welcome to our church
this Christmas;
Welcome to our church
this Christmas;
Welcome to our homes
this Christmas;
Welcome to our homes
this Christmas;
Welcome to our lives this Christmas;
Welcome to our lives this Christmas;
Lord Jesus Christ, we praise you;
Lord Jesus Christ, we praise you.

Intercessions

Pray for those who will be cold today while we sit in a warm church;

For those who will be hungry today while we look forward to good food;

For those who will be lonely today while we sit among the church family;

For those who will spend today in poverty, while others over-indulge;

For those who will be sad today, missing those they have lost;

For those who are hopeless today, not having heard the good news;

And for those who have no peace - that the Prince of peace may grant them serenity.

advent sunday

OUTLINE 10

SERVICE THEME
A song about Jesus my Saviour

CHURCH YEAR
Advent

BIBLE BASE
Luke 1:5-25,67-80

ALL-AGE SERVICE SUMMARY
This reflection on the story of Zechariah focuses on what he discovered about the role of his son, John, in God's purposes.

THIS WEEK'S RESOURCES
Create your all-age service by choosing from these resources and arranging them to suit your own situation. This outline makes use of sign language, which could provide an opportunity for someone who is hard-of-hearing to teach the congregation how to sign. Be careful about who you ask, however. Some folk are extremely sensitive on this issue.

Setting the scene

Before the service, prepare a cassette of half a dozen sounds which indicate someone or something getting ready for a significant event. Some of these involve asking someone to talk into a tape recorder; others involve recording sounds - but they are all relatively easy to achieve. Choose from the list:
1 'Ten, nine, eight, seven, six, five, four, three, two, one.' (Getting ready for a rocket to blast off.)
2 'On your marks. Get set...' (Getting ready to start a race.)
3 Instruments tuning up. (An orchestra preparing to start a concert.)
4 'Order, order!' (The speaker preparing to open proceedings in parliament.)
5 A roll of drums. (Ready for an astonishing feat of acrobatics - or the national anthem.)
6 A sequence of bell chimes: Ding-dong-ding-dong, ding-dong-ding-dong. (Big Ben in London, or a clock anywhere, preparing to strike the hour.)
7 'Going, going...' (An auctioneer about to make a sale.)
8 An organ playing the beginning of The Bridal March from *Lohengrin* by Wagner or a voice saying 'We are gathered here today, in the sight of God, to join together...' (The start of a wedding.)

At the right point in the service, announce a 'quiz' in which the congregation have to guess what important event is about to take place. Play the snatches of the tape one at a time, and ask people to call out what the noise is preparing for. Later on, we will hear about someone who had to get ready for a huge, important event - and there were no noises to help him prepare. In fact, he had to get ready for the event in complete silence.

These weeks running up to Christmas are called Advent, and they are a chance for us to get ready to meet Jesus in a wonderful way on Christmas morning. They will be full of rush and activity, but it would do us all good to have several moments along the way when we are still and quiet, remembering why we celebrate the coming of Jesus into the world. Make a point of doing so today!

A moment of stillness

Follow this introduction by singing 'Silent night'. Directly after the carol, hold a time of silence during which everyone can reflect on the preparations for Christmas to come, and ask God to make his presence known clearly despite all the rush. Bring the silence to a close by reading the words of Habakkuk 2:20:

'The Lord is in his holy temple; let all the earth be silent before him. Amen.'
(Explain what will happen before you

start to sing the hymn, so that the flow is not interrupted by announcements. Remain seated throughout to reduce disturbance and hold the silence for not more than fifteen seconds.)

Bible reading
Luke 1:5-22
Use two readers - one for the words of Gabriel, and one for everything else.

Bible teaching for all ages
Arrange the service so that the talk follows immediately after the Bible reading. Describe the nine months going by with Zechariah in a silent world unable to speak or (apparently) hear (see v62). Describe the joy he must have felt at the birth of his son, and the events of Luke 1: 57-66.

When you reach the part about Zechariah's neighbours using signs to ask him what the name of the child was to be, stop and teach the congregation how to sign the question, 'What is the name of your son?' in the manual language used today among deaf people. You will find diagrams to show how to do this on page 31. You should mouth the words as you sign them. As soon as you have taught the congregation, ask them to sign the question as if you were Zechariah and, in response, write 'His name is John' on an overhead projector or chalkboard. Read Luke 1:64 to show the remarkable events which followed.

The remainder of the talk focuses on three things which Zechariah said as part of his song in Luke 1:68-79. For each of them, teach the congregation how to sign the words in bold print below. Close by recapping the three signed sentences, with everyone doing them together. Then teach them to wish each other 'Happy Christmas' and suggest they do so before they leave the service.

God has fulfilled his promise

As far as God was concerned, there was nothing rushed or surprising about the first Christmas. He had been planning for thousands of years to send Jesus to our world. The birth of John was the final step in fulfilling his promise to send someone to save us from the mess we get ourselves into.

John prepared the way for Jesus

Zechariah's baby boy grew up to be known as John the Baptist. His task was to get people ready to meet Jesus and hear his message. He was the first person to point to Jesus, who was his cousin, and say, 'He is the one God has sent' (John 1:29,30).

Jesus brings forgiveness and peace

Why was this so important? Because Jesus coming to the world was like a bright sun rising on a land which was dark. He can drive away things which make us fearful. He can shed light on what is the right and peaceful way to live. And he brings with him the chance for our sins to be forgiven. No wonder Zechariah got so excited that he burst from silence into a song of praise to God. May you be just as thrilled as you praise God this Christmas.

Ideas for music

Choose songs and hymns about the coming of Christ and the light and hope he brings to the world.

Examples:
'Come and join the celebration'
'O come, O come Emmanuel'
"Hey! Hey! Anybody listening?"
'Silent night, holy night'
'Lift up your heads'
'Unto us a child is born'
'You are the king of glory'
'A song was heard at Christmas'
'Heaven invites you to a party'

Prayers

For the deaf or mute people

Creator God, we pray for children and adults who are not able to hear or not able to speak. Give them patience when they are frustrated, and help them as they and we learn to communicate. Keep them from danger on the road and in the home, and protect them from the thoughtless things which people say. Above all, may they take great joy in hearing you speak to them, and know the love which you silently pour out on people through Jesus Christ our Lord. Amen.

Responding to God

Invite everyone to imagine that, like Zechariah, they were not able to speak for a while. A priest's job was to lead the worship of God's people, and that is the best thing that we too can do for God. So, if words were not available to you, what would you do with your body or your movements in order to show God the love and praise that you have for him? Invite everyone to discuss the possibilities for a few seconds with those sitting next to them and to come up with an action or a movement. Then ask for silence and invite everyone to perform the action they have thought of in praise of God. While they hold the gesture there should be a few seconds of silence, and then the leader should read Luke 1:68,78,79 to bring the act of praise to a close.

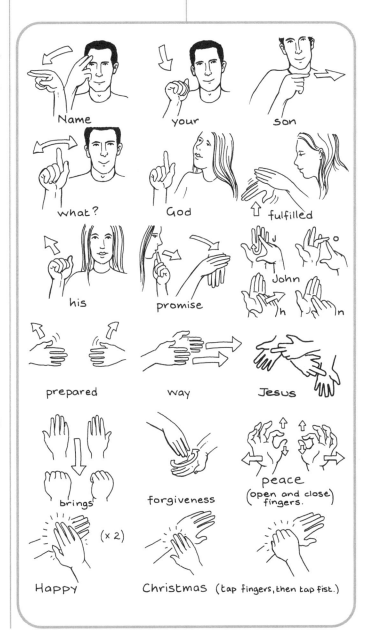

christmas

OUTLINE 11

SERVICE THEME
Hope for the world

CHURCH YEAR
Christmas

BIBLE BASE
Titus 2:11-14; Revelation 7:9-12; Matthew 2:1-16; Colossians 1:6

ALL-AGE SERVICE SUMMARY
Reflecting on and rejoicing in the different ways in which Christ, the hope for the world, is worshipped and served in various countries.

THIS WEEK'S RESOURCES
The ideas for worship in this outline assume that Christmas Day has passed and yet it is still the Christmas season. Choose items which will broaden the congregation's idea of how Christmas is celebrated and which will help them understand more of the meaning of Christ's birth. NB If using prayers in the section 'All around the world' you will need to prime people in advance.

Setting the scene

Interview someone who was born or has lived in a different country. Ask the person to describe the country, its church and its Christmas customs and to suggest items for prayer on behalf of the Christians in that country. Invite him or her to show artifacts from that country and lead the congregation in a short prayer.

Christmas game

Play the first two notes of the tune of a well-known Christmas carol and ask the congregation to guess which one it is. If the first guess is wrong, play three notes and then four, and so on. After each, ask someone to guess which country that carol comes from: 'O come all you (ye) faithful' (Italy); 'Silent night' (Austria); 'Angels from the realms of glory' (France); 'O little town of Bethlehem' (USA); 'The first Nowell' (England); 'Infant holy' (Poland).

Bible readings

Titus 2:11-14
Revelation 7:9-12
During the latter reading, ask the congregation to join the words of the crowd in verses 10 and 12. These could be written on an acetate for display on an overhead projector.

Bible teaching for all ages

Produce a large gift-wrapped box. Inside it are the items listed in italics below; invite children to dip into the box and pull out one of them. Each one is a starting-point for teaching about Christmas and the worldwide church, which can be given in any order.

A pair of swimming trunks with a scarf tied around them. Remind everyone that in many countries the weather is hot (hence the swimming trunks) or, if using this material in the southern hemisphere, cold (hence the scarf) at Christmas time. Don't forget that there are Christians all over the world all worshipping Jesus today. Read Colossians 1:6.

A shoe. In Argentina, as in many countries, presents are given, not on Christmas Day, which is a worship day, but twelve days later. Children put out their shoes in the hope that they will be filled with little gifts. This is to recall the gifts that men brought to Jesus from the east. Tell the story of Matthew 2:1-12.

A stick with a star on a string at its end. In Alaska, children play a game in which one person runs around the streets carrying the stick while others give chase and try to destroy the star. This is to remind them of Herod trying to destroy Jesus. Tell the story of Matthew 2:13-16. Then play the game!

A handful of straw. Christians in Poland put straw under the tablecloth to remind them that Jesus was laid in a manger. Remind the congregation of the changes that have taken place in Eastern Europe in the last two decades and pray for Christians in these countries.

christmas

An empty plate. Explain that while most of us eat a great deal at Christmas-time, many Christians celebrate Jesus' birth in poverty. The many Christians in Ethiopia traditionally wear brightly coloured robes when they celebrate Christmas on January 6, but often things can be very hard for them. Jesus came to earth in poverty and under the threat of violence. He must understand those who are in need today.

A tinsel 'crown' with candles. Swedish children wear these to remind them of St Lucy at Christmas. She took food to Christians hiding from persecution and wore candles on her head to leave both hands free. Invite a girl to try it on. (Give a safety warning at this point!) Don't forget that there are still many Christians who have to celebrate Christmas in secret, because their governments forbid Christians to worship Jesus.

When all the items have been shown, remind everyone that Christianity is a worldwide faith. Look forward to an 'international' heaven by reading Revelation 7:9-12.

Ideas for music

Choose songs and hymns which reflect the fact that Christmas is a celebration for people of all races and nationalities:
Examples:
'All over the world the Spirit is moving'
'Angels from the realms of glory'
'Come and join the celebration'
'Go tell it on the mountain'
'In Christ there is no east or west'
'It's rising up'
'Joy to the world the Saviour comes'
'Look to the skies, there's a celebration'
'The first Nowell'
'The light of Christ'

Prayers
All around the world
Ask everyone in the congregation to bring to church with them something that comes from another country (eg a holiday souvenir, an item of food, something electronic). Invite them to show the people sitting in front of and behind them what they have brought, and explain where it comes from. After a couple of minutes, ask them all to shout at a given signal the country that their item came from. Then quietly state: 'That country is extremely important to Jesus, for he came to earth to die for the people who live there. God bless that country. Amen.'

Intercessions
Pray for Christians in all the countries mentioned during the service, especially those who are hungry, fearful or living through political turmoil.

Later at home
Invite families to look through their food cupboards together at home and find the country of origin of the products. Then do the same with their wardrobes. Suggest that they thank God together for the food and clothes, and the fact that there are Christian sisters and brothers in that country.

mothering sunday

OUTLINE 12

SERVICE THEME
Celebrating family

CHURCH YEAR
Mothering Sunday

BIBLE BASE
Mark 1:29-34

ALL-AGE SERVICE SUMMARY
The story of Jesus healing Simon's mother-in-law is the basis of the service. As Mothering Sunday can be painful for many people, the service focuses on the whole family - all generations - and the home as a place of healing, service, welcome and where Jesus is invited in.

THIS WEEK'S RESOURCES
The service contains drama which will need to have been rehearsed by adults and those in their teens. Choose the items which are most suited to your situation.

Thanksgiving

Give everyone a pencil and a rectangle of coloured paper. Ask them to fold the top corners back so that they make a traditional house shape. This represents the place in which they live (even if it does not look much like it!). On the roof of the house they should write their name. On the body of the house they should draw themselves and the people they share their home with. They can go on to add details, such as the pets, furniture, favourite possessions, and so on.

Invite everyone to show their 'house' to the child or adult sitting next to them, and to enjoy laughing at each other's sketches, explaining what the drawings are. They should then tell that person what they are most thankful for about the home in which they live or the people with whom they share it.

While some music is played or songs are sung, the papers should be collected up by the children and brought to the front of the room. It may be possible after the service to display them with *Blu-tack* on a wall so that the prayers can be shared by anyone wanting to look at them.

Setting the scene

This short talk requires several large cardboard boxes (ask a local supermarket). Place an apparently empty one on a firm base (in fact it is not empty and has words written on the back of it, to be revealed later). Talk about the households in which we live and who might be found in them. Place other boxes on top to make a tower, each one of which bears the name of someone who makes up a household - mother, child, father, grandparent, friend, relation, lodger, pets and so on.

When the final box has been added (you will probably need to climb on a chair to do so), pretend to realise that you have mislaid something important. It is in the bottom box. Enlist someone from the congregation to help you remove that one from the pile. Ask him or her to ease the box out while you hold on to the rest.

Predictably this ends in disaster with all the boxes collapsing. Only the box at the foot of the tower remains. Turn it around. On the back are written the words: 'Supported by God'. How true - in two senses! God is a great supporter of families. He longs to see them enjoying their shared life. And it is also true that if God gets pushed out of a family's life, they lose a wonderful means of support for keeping them firm in

both bad times and good. As the Bible says: 'Children, you belong to the Lord, and you do the right thing when you obey your parents... Parents, don't be hard on your children. Raise them properly. Teach them and instruct them about the Lord.' (Ephesians 6:1-4, CEV).
Now open the box on which 'Supported by God' is written. Inside there could be flowers - enough for everyone in the congregation to give a couple to someone who has acted as a mother to them (or who has been a good friend) as a mark of appreciation and a reminder of God's love for families.

Bible reading

Mark 1:29-34

Drama

This sketch is reproduced from *Shock Tactics* by Peter Graystone, Paul Sharpe and Pippa Turner (Scripture Union), and may be photocopied for performance.

Some children do 'ave 'em!

Characters: Simon (the son), Anne, (the daughter), Ron (the father), Elsie (the mother).

Simon marches angrily around and around a table, repeatedly looking at his watch. Anne sits nervously on the edge of a chair.

Simon: It's outrageous! I can't believe they've got the nerve to disobey us again. They've got no respect.

Anne: Just calm down, Simon. Try not to be too hard on them. There might be a perfectly valid reason for them being so late.

Simon: Oh Anne, you're far too soft on them, and you shouldn't believe everything they tell you. I wonder what gem of an excuse they'll come up with tonight. We've already had, 'My watch stopped', and 'The train was late'. I offered to pick them up, but they wouldn't have it. 'Too embarrassing', they said. 'Our friends will laugh at us', they said. Well this time I've had enough. They're not going to treat this house like a hotel any more. *(He thumps the table as the front door opens. Elsie and Ron tiptoe in, giggling. Their faces drop as they see Simon and Anne waiting.)*

Anne: Simon, stay calm.

Simon: Mother, Father, come here! *(Sarcastically.)* Well, well, well! Look who we have here. And exactly what time do you call this?

Ron: Um... er... midnight, usually.

Simon: Don't try to be smart with me, old man. We told you to be home at eleven o'clock and no later. It's disgusting, people of your age being out at this time of night. You are our parents - you should be setting a good example.

Anne: Where have you been anyway?

Ron and Elsie: *(Quickly and together.)* Nowhere.

Simon: I knew it! You've been down that Conservative Club again, haven't you? *(Awkward silence.)* Speak to me when I ask you a question. Mother, have you been to the Conservative Club?

Elsie: *(Starts snivelling.)* Y...yes.

Simon: *(Getting angrier by the minute.)* I knew it! After everything we've said. Why can't you go to the Bingo Hall like nice parents?

Elsie: It's not fair. Everyone else's children let their parents go there.

Anne: *(Putting her arm around Elsie.)* Don't cry, Mum. It's just that Simon and I want what's best for you. Besides which, I don't like that Mrs Jones you meet at political meetings - she's a bad influence on you.

Elsie: *(Indignantly.)* She is not!

Anne: Don't use that tone with me, Mother. Just take a look at that awful outfit you're wearing, to prove my point. I might have guessed that when you and Mrs Jones went

shopping she'd take you to Marks and Spencer. Why didn't you get changed like I asked you to?

Simon: *(Sniffing the air around Ron.)* What's that smell, Father? I don't believe it! After all we've said - you've been drinking Horlicks again, haven't you?

Ron: Well, um, only one.

Simon: When are you going to give me some respect and start listening to what I say? You won't catch us acting like this at your age. Just... just get out of my sight before I do something that I regret.

Anne: I suggest you go straight to bed and make sure you're up early for church tomorrow.

Elsie: Oh no! Do we have to? I hate church. It's full of young people singing loud, modern songs. And the sermons are far too short. It's so irrelevant to your father and me.

Ron: I can't go anyway. I brought some work home from the office which I need to do by Monday.

Anne: Why do you always leave these things until the last minute? You should have done it on Friday night and got it out of the way.

Ron: But why?

Anne: Because... because... because I told you to. That's why! Don't argue. *(Elsie and Ron leave miserably.)*

Simon: I can see we're just going to have to be stricter with them, Anne. This isn't the 1960s any more. Just because they had to obey their parents doesn't mean they can live the wild life now. They are adults, for goodness' sake. No, while we're

living under their roof they'll have to do what we say. I'm going to have to start punishing them. *(They begin to move off, still talking.)*

Anne: I know. We could ban them from watching *Coronation Street* - that would really upset them.

Simon: Or limit Mother's hair dye allowance. She gets through far too much as it is.

Anne: That's a good idea. Oh Simon, it's so hard being somebody's children these days, don't you think?

Bible teaching for all ages

In preparation for this talk, a cassette tape needs to be made. This requires four children to talk about someone in their family - a mother, father, older brother or sister, or even a grandparent who will be in church that day. Choose carefully so as not to put a family which is already facing stress under greater pressure, and make sure that you have permission from one of the adults in the household to keep this secret from one of the others!

Ask the children you choose to describe what their relation looks like, what they enjoy most about him or her, what his or her good points are, and so on. Keep all comments positive and don't let the interview drag on for too long (thirty or forty seconds).

At the start of the talk, explain to the congregation what you have done, and ask the person who is

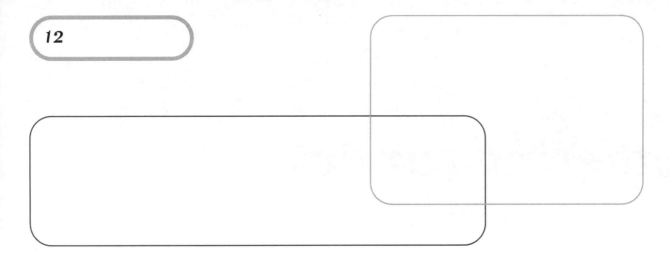

being described to come to the front of the room when they recognise themselves. Play the first interview. Enjoy the surprise and laughter. When the subject comes forward, give him or her an envelope.

Explain that inside is one of the four good things about family life as described in the Bible reading (Mark 1:29-34). Ask for the envelope to be opened and the card to be read aloud. It says: A *place of healing*. Comment on all the people who cared for Simon's mother-in-law and helped her back to health. Ask your unexpected assistant whether he or she can remember a time when someone in the family was unwell and the rest of the family helped out. You might get a monosyllabic reply or you might get an anecdote. In either case, congratulate your helper on what they have said, and encourage others to work so that their families become places where sad or sick people get better.

Play the second tape, resulting in a second person coming forward. This time the feature of good family life contained in the envelope is: A *place of service*. After the 'victim' has read this out, remind everyone that Simon's mother-in-law was so grateful for being well again that she wanted to serve everyone a meal. Ask your helper to recall a recent time when someone in the family was helpful to someone else - perhaps in the kitchen.

Continue in the same way. The third interview brings to the front someone who will read out a card saying: A *place of welcome*. Point out that the whole town was made welcome at Simon's house in order to meet Jesus, and ask whether your helper ever has guests to visit his or her home.

Play the final piece of tape. The fourth envelope contains a card which says: A *place where Jesus is invited in*. Explain that all these good things happened because Jesus was asked into the home. Inquire of your final guest whether they ever pray to Jesus as a family or whether they feel Jesus to be a part of their household.

Thank all those who have taken part, both willingly and unwillingly, and assure everyone of the care Jesus has for their family. That's a good reason to celebrate! Why not do something special together as a family, or with friends if you are single, when you get home today to mark out the day as one worth remembering?

Ideas for music

Choose songs and hymns about God's gifts to us of human relationships and of homes. Towards the end of the service, use items which invite Jesus into our lives, our homes and our community. Examples:
'Lord we come in your name'
'Now thank we all our God'
'God is our father'
'I'm your child'
'He brought me to his banqueting table'
'Jesus put this song into our hearts'
'Bind us together, Lord'
'Brother, sister, let me serve you'
'For the beauty of the earth'
'Love is his word, love is his way'

Prayers

A prayer of confession
Holy God, we confess to you the times when we have failed to treat those with whom we live with the care you expect of us.

For the things we say which will hurt each other, perfect Parent of us all,
Forgive us and help us, we pray.

For the times when we insist on getting our own way, despite what others feel, perfect Parent of us all,
Forgive us and help us, we pray.

For times when we increase the tension instead of seeking to make peace, perfect Parent of us all,
Forgive us and help us, we pray.

For our anger, our lack of respect, our failure to listen, perfect Parent of us all,
Forgive us and help us, we pray.

And because sometimes we just get bored with each other, perfect Parent of us all,
Forgive us and help us, we pray.
Amen.

Responding to God
Lord God, may my family be a place of healing, and teach me how to care for them as you do.
May my family be a place of service, and show me how to be helpful to those I live among.
May my family be a place of welcome, and may all who visit sense your love in my home.
May my family be a place where Jesus is invited in, for your presence truly gives each family something to celebrate. Amen.

Blessing
Ancient Gaelic words:

Peace between neighbours,
Peace between kindred,
Peace between lovers,
In the love of the King of Life.
Peace between person and person,
Peace between husband and wife,
Peace between parent and child,
The peace of Christ above all peace.
Amen.

mothering sunday

motherin

OUTLINE 13

SERVICE THEME
God's plan for families

CHURCH YEAR
Mothering Sunday

BIBLE BASE
2 Kings 4:1-7

ALL-AGE SERVICE SUMMARY
Taking as a starting point the story of Elisha and a poor family, the service is designed to enable the congregation to appreciate God's parental love which reaches out to people in all kinds of family situations.

THIS WEEK'S RESOURCES
The resources are not intended to fill a whole all-age service, but to give ideas as a starting point for a Mothering Sunday service.

Decoration

Around the room, place jugs, storage jars, canisters and all kinds of containers that would usually be found in a kitchen. In these flowers should be displayed, arranged practically rather than beautifully, with only a drain of water in the bottom. There should be enough flowers for every member of the congregation to take one home. The jars should be placed where children can safely reach and carry them.

Bible reading
2 Kings 4:1-7

While this is being read, a woman could mime collecting jars and pouring oil into one after the other.

Bible teaching for all ages

Begin by inviting all the children under about ten years old to sit on the floor at the front of the room to listen to a story. Retell the Bible story, explaining how a mother whose husband had died finds God supplying her needs through the help of Elisha, her sons and her neighbours. Show a small jar of olive oil as an illustration.

At the point in the story where the widow needs empty jars, look around the room as if searching for something suitable to represent these. When you notice (as if by surprise!) the jugs and cans containing flowers, ask all the children to help you by collecting them from around the room. When they have been brought to the front, take out the flowers and use the jars as you mime pouring olive oil.

Make three points:

1 The story is a lovely one for Mothering Sunday, since it is full of people who care for each other. But most of all, it shows how God cares for all kinds of families, from the richest to the poorest.

2 You don't have to be a 'Happy Families' family with a mother, father, son and daughter in order to be special to God. The family in the story had one mum and two sons. Today God wants to tell you how special you are - if you are a mother, or a father, if your children have grown up and left home, if you are single, if your mum and dad are not with you in church today, if you don't have the children you wish you had - whoever you are.

3 Just as the children and the mother in the story worked together so that God could work a miracle, so God longs for families today to help and support each other. Even Elisha had his part to play in the life of the family. This is how God's plans for families today can best be fulfilled. Suggest that the children give out the flowers all around the church. If their mother is with them, it would be good to take her one first. Then they give them to anyone, male or female, who would like them or take them to anyone at home who might appreciate them.

mothering sun

thering sunday

Ideas for music

Choose songs and hymns about love between people of all ages.
Examples:
'A naggy mum, a grumpy dad'
'For the beauty of the earth'
'Jesus put this song into our hearts'
'Let there be love'
'Turn the hearts of the children'
'Father God I wonder'
'I'm special'

Prayers

Praising God

A prayer for two leaders, with a congregational response based on Isaiah 66:13; 49:15; Psalm 131:2; Matthew 23:37:

A: In the Bible, Isaiah speaks of God as a mother, caring and comforting us like a child in arms.
B: Marvellous God, who loves us as a mother,
All: We your children give you praise.
A: God could no more forget us than a mother could forget her children.
B: Marvellous God who loves us as a mother,
All: We your children give you praise.
A: David wrote that in God's presence he is quiet and at peace, like a child who feels safe with her mother.
B: Marvellous God who loves us as a mother,
All: We your children give you praise.
A: Jesus spoke of his motherly love, longing to shield us like a mother hen's wings around her chicks.
B: Marvellous God who loves us as a mother,
All: We your children give you praise.

Prayer for families

Lord Jesus, you know what it is like to live in a family.
We pray for all the families of this church.

palm sunday

palm sund

SERVICE THEME
Are you the King of the Jews?

CHURCH YEAR
Palm Sunday

BIBLE BASE
John 12:12-16; 18:28 - 19:16

ALL-AGE SERVICE SUMMARY
The service begins with material for Palm Sunday, but moves the story of Jesus' final week forward to include his trial in order to provide an opportunity to think about parts of the gospel which may be less familiar to people who will not be in church again until Easter Sunday.

THIS WEEK'S RESOURCES
The Bible teaching for this outline takes the form of a narrative with prayers and other activities interspersed among the sections. Other items of prayer and music should precede and follow this.

Setting the scene

Invite young children to join you at the front of the room and produce two sacks full of objects. They contain pairs of objects, and will be part of a game which involves matching the pairs. Firstly, open one of the sacks and get out the objects - a canister of salt, a fork, a screw, a camera, a bicycle tyre, a set of head-phones (obviously these objects can be varied to suit what is available, except for the important one which is...) a piece of gold (a stone sprayed gold for the less opulent!). Give each of these to a different adult to hold. Now open the second sack, and ask the children to help you sort out who to give each item to. In this sack there should be a pepper mill, a spoon, a screwdriver, a reel of film, a bicycle pump, a personal stereo, and (again this is the important one...) a crown of thorns (a branch twisted into a circle). The first six should be easy to match and can be done in any order. But what about the strange combination that is left - a lump of gold and a thorny crown? Actually, they do belong together, as we shall find out later during the coming week. They belong together because they both belong to a king. Strange! Do you remember that at Christmas, a long time ago now, we heard about wise men visiting the infant Jesus? What did they bring? Yes, gold! Gold, because they recognised Jesus to be king. And why does that belong with this

branch of thorns? Well, Jesus never wore a gold crown, even though he is King of all heaven and earth. The crown he wore was a cruel one made of spikes and brambles. He is a different kind of king from the one anyone expected. So we will praise Jesus the King as we hear today's story - because Jesus and worship belong together like salt and pepper.

Bible reading
John 18:28 - 19:16

On this occasion it is suggested that the reading is incorporated into the Bible teaching and worship suggestions given below. It could be arranged for three readers - Pilate, Jesus and a narrator (who also reads the words attributed to the crowd or the Jewish authorities). Small pieces of connecting narrative such as 'Pilate said' could be omitted. At

19:9, replace the words, 'But Jesus did not answer' with a silence.

Bible teaching and worship

Everyone should be given, as they enter the building, a sheet (folded) from a recent newspaper. For manageability, it is probably better to give adults a page from a broadsheet and children a sheet from a tabloid (but remove any pages which would be likely to cause an unhelpful distraction from worship). If you are able to use newspapers that have a children's supplement, so much the better.

Intercession

In a time of intercession, ask people to call out from their pages things that are going on in the world which God must be concerned about. Make

palm sunday

a list of them, and then pray about those situations.

Activity
Subsequently, ask everyone to take their sheet of newspaper, fold in half, and tear it from it the open ends toward the fold. They should tear most of the way up but leave about 15 cm at the folded side (the diagram on page 39 makes this clear - it might help to explain the effect you want by comparison to a grass skirt). They should then roll it into a tube, so that the untorn edge becomes a handle to hold it by and the torn parts look a little like leaves.

Narrative and song
Tell the story of Jesus' entry into Jerusalem from John 12:12-16. Go on to sing 'Make way, make way'. Every time the refrain comes around, encourage everyone to play the part of the Passover crowd coming out of the gates of Jerusalem to welcome their King and to wave the symbolic 'palms' that they have made, in a broad sweep from side to side.

Narrative and reading
Then talk about the way in which public opinion turned against Jesus during the week that followed; about the way the religious leaders turned the people against him; and the way he was finally arrested and brought to trial. At this point, read John 18:28 - 19:16 in the way described above. When the crowd is represented as angry, ask the congregation to shake their 'branches' angrily as though they were whips (ie 18:40 and 19:15).

Song and talk
Follow this with another hymn, 'Were you there when they crucified my Lord?' Sing the first three verses. This time, whenever the word 'tremble' comes in the song,

everyone should rustle the newspaper 'palms' as if they were trembling in sympathy and awe. After three verses, remind the congregation of the things from the newspapers that they prayed about earlier. Make the connections that it is because of the wrong things in the world that Jesus had to come to earth and suffer so terribly. But as we shall all hear next week, Jesus, overcoming all the evil that was directed against him, rose again from the dead. This means that we can live with the sure hope that good will overcome evil in our world through the final intervention of God. Close this section by singing the final verse: 'Were you there when God raised him from the dead?' with branches raised high in praise of the living King Jesus.

Ideas for music
Choose songs and hymns written for Palm Sunday or those which look forward to the kingship of Christ or reflect on his suffering.
Examples:
'Hosanna, hosanna'
'Lift up your heads'
'Ride on, ride on in majesty'
'He walked where I walk'
'Blessing and honour' (Ancient of Days)
'Jesus is the name we honour'
'We have a king who rides on a donkey'
'All glory, laud (praise) and honour'

Prayers
Welcoming Jesus
Jesus, ride into our universe,
We welcome you here as King.
Jesus, ride on to this planet,
We welcome you here as King.
Jesus, ride throughout our nation,
We welcome you here as King.
Jesus, ride into (name of your town),
We welcome you here as King.
Jesus, ride up this street,
We welcome you here as King.
Jesus, ride into our church,
We welcome you here as King.
Jesus, ride into my life,
We welcome you here as King.
King of the universe, King of our nation, King of this church, my King,
We welcome you here as King.

Procession
Use some of the objects which have featured in this service as part of a procession. First of all, three or four people walk from the back of the room to the front carrying branches (either the newspaper ones, or ones made from green paper, or real ones). During this, joyful music should be played. The branches are placed on a table. The music stops and the leader reads the words: 'Do not be afraid. See your king is coming, riding on a donkey. Hosanna! Blessed is he who comes in the name of the Lord.'
There is a sudden change of atmosphere as a slow drum beat starts. A second group of people come forward, bearing the crown of thorns and a piece of gold. These are

also placed on the table, with the words: 'Here is the man. We despised him and rejected him. He endured the suffering that should have been ours. We are healed by the punishment that he suffered; made whole by the blows he received. See him come.'
This could be followed with the song, 'See him come, the king upon a donkey'.

Confession
When we know what is good, but fail to do it, Lord forgive us.
Forgive us and help us.
When we buzz with enthusiasm, then let people down, Lord forgive us.
Forgive us and help us.
When anger leads to us doing things we regret, Lord forgive us.
Forgive us and help us.
When we take the short cut because the right thing is too hard, Lord forgive us.
Forgive us and help us.
When we let injustice continue and don't say a word, Lord forgive us.
Forgive us and help us.
For being like Pilate, being like the disciples, being like the crowd, being like Peter, being like Judas, Lord forgive us.
Forgive us and help us.

palm sunday

palm sunday

OUTLINE 15

SERVICE THEME
Who is Jesus?

CHURCH YEAR
Palm Sunday

BIBLE BASE
Matthew 21:1-11; John 12:17-36

ALL-AGE SERVICE SUMMARY
The service begins with Jesus' entry into Jerusalem and goes on to explore Jesus' claims about himself in order to give answers to the question of who Jesus is.

THIS WEEK'S RESOURCES
Choose items which relate directly to the entry into Jerusalem for the beginning (and possibly the conclusion) of the service; those which relate to John 12:17-36 are intended for the central part of worship.

Setting the scene

You will need a helium balloon on a string (or perhaps several). Talk about how exciting occasions are often marked with balloons. Birthdays, weddings, anniversaries, welcomes... all of them may be decorated with balloons. Today everyone is going to hear about a very exciting day in Jesus' life. Of course, balloons weren't invented in his day, so instead the people festooned the place with... well, telling you would give the game away, so you can find out later! On that day, everyone was asking 'Who is he? Who is he? Who is he?' Different people had different theories. Was he a new king for Israel? Was he a magician who could do great wonders? Or was he just a nuisance? Take a felt marker and write on the balloon 'Who'. Turn the balloon and start to add a question mark, but as you do so let go of it, as if by accident. Watch as it ascends to the ceiling. When it gets there say, 'Too late now!'

Jesus knew his time was running out too. He wanted people to think about who he claimed to be and to follow him before it was too late. Sadly, many did leave it too late and missed the opportunity to worship him as God while he was still with them. We don't have the chance to question Jesus in person because, like the balloon, he is not with us any more. But from heaven, where he has ascended, he still wants us to

find out who he is. He is longing for us to worship him as God. We have the chance to consider his exciting claims today. Don't leave it too late or the chance might slip out of your grasp!

Bible reading
Matthew 21:1-11

This story should be read early in the service, the congregation joining in with the words of the crowd which could be written up on an overhead projector or on a service sheet. A cue should be given at the appropriate moment.

John 12:17-26

This should be read before the Bible teaching section with an explanation that these stories are written in John's Gospel directly after the story of Jesus' entry into Jerusalem.

Bible teaching for all ages

This talk requires several visual aids. You need three large boxes. Cover them in decorative paper and write on the front of them, one word per box: Who Are You? Line up the letters so that downwards they spell 'way' if the boxes are piled on top of each other. Inside the first box place a battered cardboard crown. Inside the second put a spoon, a candle (and matches), some cooking oil and corn kernels of the kind which are used to make popcorn. The third contains a torch (or perhaps a

lantern which could be lit with a candle).

Remind everyone that today's reading was about some people who came to Jesus wanting to know who he was. This would not be surprising were it not for the fact that they were foreigners, not Jews at all, and it was a sign that Jesus' message was about to spread further than it had ever reached before. Encourage the congregation to join in this talk by saying, 'Who are you, Jesus?' every time one of the boxes is lifted high. Have a practice, and then go on to talk about three signs that Jesus gave to show who he was. None of them were a straightforward answer, but all of them explained a lot. For each one, open one of the boxes and take out the visual aid that goes with it.

A king on a donkey

Show the crown and explain that the way that Jesus came into Jerusalem reminded people, years later, of the way their long-expected leader, the Messiah, was to be recognised. They did not understand it at the time, but it did not stop them greeting him like a king. They knew that they were in the presence of someone who performed remarkable miracles and wanted to know, 'Who are you Jesus?' Read John 12:17-19

A seed that came alive

Place a tiny amount of oil in the

spoon, put a corn kernel on it, and hold the candle underneath. If you can do this and talk at the same time, the congregation will pay close attention, and will be waiting for the corn to spring out of the spoon. (It is wise to practise!) When the Greeks asked, 'Who are you, Jesus?' he answered with a strange parable - about a seed that died but came alive. That is what all seeds do - by being buried in the ground they create new life for hundreds of others. Jesus knew that the time of his death was near, but that he would spring to life again so that countless millions of people would live for ever too. Read verse 24 (or get someone else to read it if you are still waiting for the corn to pop!).

A light in the darkness
All this talk about Jesus dying confused the crowds who had come to see Jesus. They wanted someone to follow for ever. Out of their confusion, they asked, 'Who are you, Jesus? So he described himself as a light. (Get out the torch or light the lantern.) On a dark night, you can trust this to show you where it is good and safe to walk. That is why Jesus went on to compare himself to a light - he came to show us the way to live which was good and safe. He urged people to follow the example of his way of life before it was too late. Read verses 35,36a.

Conclusion
Pile up the boxes on top of each other (prompting the congregation to join in each time). When you have done so, point out the word 'way' which has been formed. Read verse 26a and remind the congregation that Jesus' claim to be a king, a living seed and a light, demands a response - who will follow in his way?

Ideas for music
Choose songs and hymns written for Palm Sunday and those which remind us of the kingship of Jesus or look ahead to his death and resurrection.
Examples:
'Ride on, ride on in majesty'
'Welcome, king of kings'
'Going up to Jerusalem'
'Hosanna, hosanna'
'King of kings and Lord of lords'
'We want to see Jesus lifted high'
'Lift up your heads to the coming king'
'You are the king of glory'
'Come on and celebrate'
'Make way, make way'

Credal song
In response to the theme of the service, sing the oldest creed known to the Christian community. It should be sung to the tune (rhythm modified as needed) 'Frère Jacques'. Firstly sing it to establish the tune, then as a round, dividing the congregation into up to four sections:

Christ has died, Christ has died;
Christ has risen, Christ has risen;
Christ will come again, Christ will come again;
He's my Lord, he's my Lord.

Prayers
Psalm praise
A setting of Psalm 118:19,24,26-29 for leader and congregation response:

Open the gates, I want to come in,
I will give thanks to the Lord.
This is the day that the Lord has made,
I will give thanks to the Lord.
Let us rejoice and be glad today,
I will give thanks to the Lord.
Blessed is he who comes in God's name,
I will give thanks to the Lord.
God is our Lord and light shines on us,
I will give thanks to the Lord.
With palms in our hands and a festival song,
I will give thanks to the Lord.
You are our God and we glorify you,
I will give thanks to the Lord.
God's love will go on for ever and ever,
I will give thanks to the Lord.

Praise God! Hosanna!
Use this shout of praise to God which uses various verses from the psalms. Perhaps the congregation could wave their overcoats or sweaters or shake their handkerchiefs to accompany it.

Proclaim with me the Lord's greatness,
Praise God! Hosanna!
Praise his name, all you who obey him,
Praise God! Hosanna!
Praise the Lord, for he is a great king,
Praise God! Hosanna!
He rules over the whole earth,
Praise God! Hosanna!
For those who honour the Lord, his love lasts for ever,
Praise God! Hosanna!
God bless him who comes in the name of the Lord,
Praise God! Hosanna!

holy week

maundy thursday - a family communion

communio

OUTLINE 16

SERVICE THEME
A way of remembering Jesus

CHURCH YEAR
Holy week – a family
Communion

BIBLE BASE
Mark 14:12-26

ALL-AGE SERVICE SUMMARY
The content of the service links
Christian Communion with the
celebration of Passover in the
Old and New Testaments. Drama
for three characters is included
(the actors need to be able to
learn lines and speak audibly).

THIS WEEK'S RESOURCES
The suggested activities can be
used to supplement the normal
practice of your church for the
celebration of Communion. It
can be used as a means of
helping members of the
congregation (not only children)
to understand more about the
meaning and origins of
Communion. It should be
decided beforehand how to
include those who do not
normally take Communion and
this should be explained simply
during the service.

Setting the scene
To highlight the theme of
remembering, hold a quiz which
uncovers what people remember
abut the story of the Exodus,
perhaps between two teams of
children and adults who volunteer to
take part. When the questions are
finished, make a comparison
between us trying to remember a
story we've heard comparatively
recently and the Israelites needing to
remember it for hundreds of years.
How did they remember? By eating
the same meal that their ancestors
ate the night of their escape every
year as a celebration. How have
Christians remembered what Jesus
did almost two thousand years ago?
They too have a special celebration
meal, as we shall all see today.

Q1. In what country were the
Israelites slaves?
A. Egypt.
Q2. Who took Moses into his family
when he was on the run?
A. Jethro.
Q3. What was the unique name for
himself that God revealed to Moses
at the burning bush?
A. Yahweh (or Jehovah) or 'I am'.
Q4. What was the name of the meal
that the Israelites ate the night that
they escaped?
A. The Passover.
Q5. As they escaped, how did the
Israelites know which way to go?
A. They followed pillars of fire and
cloud.

Q6. Which sea parted to allow the
Israelites to get away from their
enemies?
A. The Red Sea (or Sea of Reeds).

Bible reading
Mark 14:12-26
A woman could read the narration
and a man read the words of Jesus.

Bible teaching for all ages
If the talk takes place before
Communion is celebrated, use as a
visual aid the bread and wine that
will later be the elements. If not,
display an unleavened loaf, a pitcher
of wine and Passover foods (lamb,
herbs, salt water and so on) as you
speak. The illustrations shown on
page 44 should help you as well.
Divide the talk into three sections.

Remembering the past
The night before he died, Jesus
celebrated the Passover, as he would
have done many times before. As all
Jewish men were expected to at the
time, Jesus celebrated in Jerusalem
with his disciples. It would have
brought back memories of how God
set free their ancestors during a
bleak time in their history.

Understanding the present
The disciples would have been taken
completely by surprise when Jesus
gave a new significance to the bread
and wine. He was trying to help
them understand that the suffering

he was about to go through was on
their behalf - and on our behalf.

Preparing for the future
Jesus asked his followers to repeat
the action of eating bread and
drinking wine again and again so
that we would never forget that he
lived, died and rose again. And that
is exactly what has happened in
Communion services throughout
history and across the world.
(Describe the practice in your own
church.) It will go on happening
until Jesus comes back in person.

Drama
This sketch is for two women and
one man. At the beginning the two
women are washing up supposedly
whilst the Last Supper is taking place
in a room above. As characters exit
and return, they are carrying dishes
to serve as part of the Passover or
bringing plates to be washed.

Anna: Phew! This washing up is
going on forever. However many are
there upstairs?
Rhoda: Thirteen apparently. Haven't
you peeped in?
Anna: Of course not. I've been too
busy down here preparing the
Passover food and washing up the
bowls.
Rhoda: Well, you're doing a great
job. There's something odd about the
atmosphere up there. Those Passover
meals are usually full of celebration
and laughter. This one seems a bit

a family communion

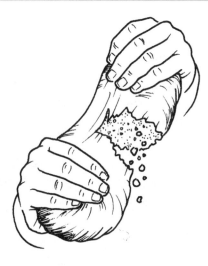

heavy-hearted.

Anna: Well, it obviously hasn't affected their appetite.

Rhoda: You're right. Here's another dish.

Anna: I had a dream last night that one day in the future there will be a machine, and you would just put the dishes in, add water, press a button and - whoosh - an hour later they would all be clean! *(They roar with laughter.)*

Rhoda: Yes, yes, that's possible.

Anna: And I dreamt that people wouldn't eat with their fingers, but with dainty little implements. *(Laughter.)*

Rhoda: I don't see why not.

Anna: And that there would be this soapy liquid in a container that would make washing up ten times easier. *(Laughter again.)*

Rhoda: Possible! Possible!

Anna: And I dreamt that men would do just as much washing up as women. *(They are just about to laugh when they catch sight of each other.*

They shake their heads.)

Rhoda: Oh now, that is ridiculous! *(Enter Mark.)*

Mark: They're ready for the next jug of wine. Come on now, Rhoda. No messing. *(Exit Rhoda, carrying jug.)* Is all well?

Anna: Yes, sir. Tell me, how do they come to be celebrating the Passover here?

Mark: They've come down from Galilee with the rabbi, Jesus. I met them by the city gates when I was fetching water from the well - water which you should have been collecting.

Anna: Yes, sir. I know sir. Thank you, sir.

Mark: Two of them, there were! Followed me here and spoke to the governor. He was obviously expecting them because the room was ready. They have been here all day preparing for the meal. Apparently there was some fuss because I wasn't there to wash their feet as they arrived. Don't look at me

like that! I didn't know. I wasn't asked!

Anna: Is there trouble about it, sir?

Mark: Not with me. Jesus did it instead. Goodness knows why he wants to do the servant's job, but he doesn't seem proud about that kind of thing. I only hope I don't get a beating from the governor for it. *(Enter Rhoda.)*

Rhoda: Sir, the bread, sir.

Mark: I'm going. *(He exits, taking a plate of bread with him.)*

Rhoda: Anna, there's something very odd there. The mood isn't just heavy-hearted. It's...

Anna: It's what?

Rhoda: I don't know. You know how the Jews eat the Passover every year so that they will never forget being rescued from slavery in Egypt.

Anna: Vaguely.

Rhoda: Well they do. It's all very symbolic. They have bitter herbs to represent how harsh their treatment was as slaves, and salt water to remind them of their tears. And that

lamb we took in earlier is the same meal that they ate the night before their escape - when their God rescued them. They have eaten the same meal every year since, and it's always a thankful and happy time.

Anna: And this isn't?

Rhoda: Well... what do you think?

Anna: I don't think anything. I just do washing up.

Rhoda: They were talking about betrayal up there. It's like their leader is saying goodbye to them. He's talking like something awful is about to happen. Here comes Mark. *(Enter Mark, distracted. The women stop chatting and set to work again.)* What should I take up now, sir? *(No response.)*

Anna: Sir?

Mark: Er... yes?

Rhoda: Is it bread or wine that they have next?

Mark: Um... I don't know. This is not like a normal Passover.

Rhoda: *(Under her breath to Anna.)* Told you.

communio

Mark: He took the bread, just like you'd expect.

Anna: Who did?

Mark: Jesus did, but he didn't say what they normally say. *(The women are leaning forward to listen, but Mark is thinking too hard to notice.)*

Anna: And?

Mark: And what?

Rhoda: What did he say, sir?

Mark: He said, 'This is my body and I am giving it for you. Take it and eat it.'

Anna: Eating bodies?

Mark: No, not like that. He said, 'Every time you eat like this, remember me.' And then when it came to drinking the wine, he said, 'This wine is my blood, which I am pouring out for you. It seals God's covenant.'

Anna: Scary!

Mark: No. It wasn't scary at all. It was... reassuring. It was unforgettable.

Rhoda: Are you sure those were the words?

Mark: Of course I'm sure. I'm never going to forget them.

Anna: Is that music I can hear?

Rhoda: They're singing a hymn.

Mark: The meal is over. I heard them say they are going to... I don't know... some garden somewhere.

Anna: Oh well, that's another evening over. They may have had a strange conversation, but there is nothing strange about the number of dirty dishes. *(Mark goes to leave.)*

Anna: What would you like us to do now, sir?

Mark: Er... nothing. Leave it. I'll finish this when I get back.

Rhoda: What did you say? Are you feeling all right, sir?

Anna: Are you going out?

Mark: Yes, I thought I would follow them. Just to see Jesus...

Anna: To see Jesus do what?

Mark: Just to see what happens if I follow.

Anna: Aren't you going to take your cloak? It's a cold night.

Mark: I can't spare the time to fetch it or I'll lose them.

Rhoda: Don't get into trouble. They were talking as if something fearful is about to occur.

Anna: And let us know what happens, Mark. If you don't get arrested on the way!

Mark: I've got a pretty fast pair of legs. *(He goes to leave, then turns around.)* Thank you. *(Exit. The women look at each other astonished.)*

Anna: Rhoda, that's the first time a man has ever said thank you to me.

Rhoda: Well... tonight certainly is a night to remember!

Ideas for music

Choose songs and hymns concerned with the celebration of communion. Examples:

'Broken for me'
'I am the bread of life'
'Jesus Christ, I think upon your sacrifice' (Once again)
'O what a gift!'
'Take, eat'
'Take this bread I give'

Prayers

Intercessions

Look back over the past year, remembering what God has done in your church since last Easter, and thank him. Pray for all those who will celebrate Communion in secret today because they cannot worship openly, those who cannot join with you to do so because they are ill, and that those who will celebrate Passover this year without realising who Jesus is may come to recognise him as Lord.

Pre-Communion prayer

If children will be present when Communion is celebrated, invite them to gather or sit around the table and join in this prayer. An adult prayer of consecration could then follow.

Leader: Here is a loaf of bread.
Children: We will remember Jesus.
Leader: Here is a cup of wine.
Children: We will remember Jesus.
Leader: Watch as the bread is broken.
Children: We will remember Jesus.
Leader: Watch as the wine is poured.
Children: We will remember Jesus.
Leader: Now the bread will be eaten.
Children: We will remember Jesus.

Remembering

Invite children and adults to make clusters of two or three and between them remember some of the things that Jesus did. After a minute or two, proclaim them as part of an act of praise. Either encourage people to call out what they thought of so that the leader can mention them all in one prayer, or hold a time of open prayer, inviting people to praise Jesus for what he did.

good friday

good friday

OUTLINE 17

SERVICE THEME
Why is it called Good Friday?

CHURCH YEAR
Good Friday

BIBLE BASE
John 19:16-30

ALL-AGE SERVICE SUMMARY
This is a conventional, but appropriately restrained, all-age service which focuses on the truth that the death of Jesus, though seemingly bad, brings untold good to people for eternity.

THIS WEEK'S RESOURCES
The resources reflect the likelihood of very young children being present. Choose those items which will fit in well with your own tradition's style for Good Friday.

Greeting

Invite everyone to reflect on the fact that Jesus' death on the cross has opened the way for evil to be overcome finally by good. Suggest that they assure each other of this by moving around the church greeting the people they know (if they are children) and also people they do not know (if they are adults). They should draw a sign of the cross with their finger on the palm of the people they greet, saying 'May Jesus make this a Good Friday for you.'

Dramatic Bible reading

John 19:16-30

As the reading progresses, adults and children, representing different characters, could approach a cross set up at the front of the building. (Use one which is permanently there, if possible.) There is no need to have anyone to represent Jesus, the two men could be standing either side of the cross, heads down (the others who were crucified with him); Pilate bearing a placard saying: 'Jesus of Nazareth, King of the Jews'; a group to represent the chief priests who stand between Pilate and the cross, then walk away and stand with their backs to the cross; soldiers who bring on a white sheet bundled up and sit rolling dice; four women and girls and a young man, all weeping. None of the characters need be in costume. As the reader says Jesus' last words: 'It is finished', all turn to look up at the cross and freeze until the reading is over. There should be a fifteen second pause before the last sentence of the reading.

Bible teaching for all ages

In order to give this talk, you will need to have transferred on to acetate the pictures inside letters on page 47. (Make sure that you use acetates that will not melt inside a photocopier. These can be found in any office or art shop.) Cut them into individual letters so that they can be arranged on an OHP in three different ways:

bad

Why is today called Good Friday? It is the day when we remember the terrible suffering of a good man. Why not 'Bad Friday'? Pilate and the Jewish leaders thought it was a good Friday, because it seemed that the death of Jesus solved their problems. They thought it proved that Jesus was not from God. But when he rose again on Easter Sunday, it was the very reverse!

god

(Remove the b and a, and replace them with the g and the o which shows a woman's face.) For the soldiers it was neither a bad nor a good day - just a day's work. For the family of Jesus, it was a dreadful day, because they experienced the suffering that so many do today when someone they love dies. However, it was no ordinary man who they were mourning; it was God himself. That makes a difference to all Christians going through times of sadness today, because the God we worship has been through anguish just like us, so we are never suffering alone.

good

(Add the o which shows a modern-day group.) Is it Good Friday for us? Yes, it is, for the death of Jesus meant that human beings could become friends of God and live with him in heaven where suffering will end for ever. It is a place where good things will happen to all people! That is not just good news; it is wonderful news! Perhaps the name of Good Friday should be changed - not to Bad Friday, but to Best Friday!

Ideas for music

Choose songs and hymns on the theme of the cross, taking care to ensure that the meaning of the words are clear and easily understood by children or those who do not normally attend church services.

good friday

Examples:

'It is a thing most wonderful'
'There is a green hill far away'
'I'm special'
'Oh how he loves you and me'
'At the foot of the cross'
'Thank you, Jesus, thank you, Jesus'
'There is a redeemer'
'Lord, I lift your name on high'
'My Lord, what love is this?'
'When I survey the wondrous cross'

Prayers

Intercessions

Lord God, we bring before you the suffering of our world;
The sick and injured in their pain;
The starving in their weakness;
The aged in their frailty;
The war-torn in their agony;
The homeless in their vulnerability;
The prisoners in their sighing;
The refugees in their wandering;
The bereaved in their grieving;
The broken-hearted in their loneliness;
The mentally ill in their confusion;
The addicted in their helplessness.
Comfort them in their distress,
And bring them by way of the cross,
To the hope of the new life that only resurrection can bring,
Through Jesus Christ who shares the world's pain. Amen.

Prayer of thanks

Lord Jesus, I'm sad that wicked men treated you so cruelly;
I'm sad that you were beaten and mocked;
I'm sad that your friends ran away and left you;
I'm sad that you were nailed to a cross and left to die;
I'm sad that you didn't even have a grave of your own, but a borrowed one;
But I'm glad, very glad, wonderfully glad that you came alive again and will never die.
Thank you, Lord Jesus, for bearing it all for my sake. Amen.

good friday

od friday

OUTLINE 18

SERVICE THEME
Shall I crucify your king?

CHURCH YEAR
Good Friday

BIBLE BASE
John 19:14–30

ALL-AGE SERVICE SUMMARY
A meditation with action and prayer on the Passion of Jesus, God himself suffering at the hands of his creation.

THIS WEEK'S RESOURCES
This act of worship is in six parts. Each part is focused on an object mentioned in John 19, which is physically represented at the service. The resources should be used in a serious but spirited way – reasonably fast-moving. The drama, if you decide to use it, would fit best at the end of the service, before a final hymn.

The crown of thorns

Suggested song: *'O sacred head sore wounded/surrounded'*
Reading: John 19:1-6
Procession: Slowly and in silence, a crown of thorns is brought from the back of the room, up an aisle, and is placed on a table at the front. This contribution to the service could be done effectively by young children. The crown of thorns needs only to be a home-made article made from a twisted branch. (Thought should be given in advance as to where the objects will be placed in relation to each other.)
Comment: Talk about the route Jesus had taken in a matter of days from a king welcomed with cloaks spread before him to a king insulted with a mock crown. It was God himself who was ridiculed in that vicious crown.
A time of silence may be kept. This is particularly appropriate and could be prolonged if the congregation is predominantly adult. At an all-age service, however, a few seconds of silence is sufficient, and the noise of toddlers should be accepted as part of their worship rather than a problem.
Prayer: A prayer from the Orthodox Paschal cycle:

Today he who hung the earth upon the waters is hung upon the cross;
He who is king of the angels is arrayed in a crown of thorns;
He who wraps the heaven in clouds is wrapped in the purple of mockery;
He who, at his baptism set Adam free, receives blows upon his face;
The bridegroom of the church is transfixed with nails;
The son of a virgin is pierced with a spear;
We venerate your passion, O Christ;
Show us also thy glorious resurrection.

The nails

Suggested songs: *'He was pierced for our transgressions'* or *'Come and see'*
Reading: John 19:14-18
Procession: Three large nails are brought from the back of the room and laid next to the crown of thorns.
Comment: Nails were familiar to Jesus – a carpenter's workshop is always stocked with nails. But now, the nails which in Jesus' hands had been used creatively, were turned against him to be used cruelly – in Jesus' hands. It was God himself whose hands were pierced with nails.
A time of silence may be kept.
Prayer: O Jesus, we watch with shame as you are nailed cruelly to the cross.
We watch with shame for our actions which have distressed others;
Lord Jesus forgive us.
We watch with shame for our words which have grieved others;
Lord Jesus we are sorry.
We watch with shame for our thoughts which have diminished others;
Lord Jesus have mercy.
We nail to the cross all that we have done wrong,
Asking you to take it away and lead us into a better life. Amen.

The sign

Suggested songs: *'Man of sorrows'* or *'He walked where I walk'*
Reading: John 19:19-22
Procession: A piece of wood on which is roughly painted 'The King of the Jews' is added to the other objects on the table.
Comment: It was quite usual for a criminal to hang under a sign that accused him of his crime: 'thief", 'deserter'. But surely no one had seen a sign like this before: 'The King of the Jews'. Why do you suppose Pilate insisted that it said that? He had asked, 'Shall I crucify your king?' It was God himself who hung under the sign 'King of the Jews'.
A time of silence may be kept.
Prayer: Lord Jesus, for those today who suffer like you - entirely unfairly - we weep.
For those who are behind bars because they stood for justice, we weep;
For those who are separated from their families because they could not let evil go unchallenged, we weep;
For those who are tortured because they spoke out against what is wrong, we weep;
For those whose loved ones have disappeared with no trace, we weep;
For the torturers and jailers and tyrant and oppressors, we weep,
Because for them the day of reckoning is bound to come.

The robe

Suggested songs: *'A purple robe'* or *'I'm special'*
Reading: John 19: 1-3, 23-27
Procession: A piece of purple material is brought to the front of the room and draped over the table next to other objects.
Comment: Purple is a fine colour and purple cloth was expensive in Jesus' time. It was the right colour for mockery! I don't suppose the

clothes that Jesus wore on his final journey were purple. At the end, they were the only things he owned. It was God himself whose very clothes were divided and gambled for.

A time of silence may be kept.

Prayer: Clothe me, Lord Jesus, with your protection to keep danger from me;
Clothe me, Lord Jesus, with your hope to keep doubt from me;
Clothe me, Lord Jesus, with your light to keep darkness from me;
Clothe me, Lord Jesus, with your peace to keep evil from me;
Wrap me, Lord Jesus, in the seamless love of the cross. Amen.

The drink

Suggested songs: 'On Calvary's tree' or 'How deep the Father's love for us'
Reading: John 19:28-30
Procession: A ceramic bowl filled with vinegar is placed on the table.
Comment: In the last minutes of his life, Jesus was desperate to say something, but he was too dry and tired to get the words out. In one of the few acts of kindness shown toward Jesus in these awful hours, he was offered a drink. What was it he wanted to say? A triumphant whisper: 'I have done what I came to do'? It was God himself who had come to this earth and died.

A time of silence may be kept.

Prayer: The prayer of Richard of Chichester:

Thanks be to you, my Lord Jesus Christ,
For all the benefits which you have given us;
For all the pains and insults which you have borne for us;
O most merciful redeemer, friend and brother,
May we know you more clearly,
Love you more dearly,
Follow you more nearly, day by day. Amen.

The spear

Suggested songs: 'When I survey the wondrous cross' or 'At the foot of the cross'
Reading: John 19:31-35
Procession: The spear could be

represented by a wooden broomstick (do not attempt to disguise it).
Comment: It is impossible to end this sad service without looking forward to Easter, when Jesus was raised from the dead and made Lord of all. The wound of that dreadful spear was a symbol of death. But the death of Jesus on a cross was a symbol of healing. Wrongdoing is healed by forgiveness; enmity with God is healed by love; death is healed for ever by Jesus' triumph. It was God himself who did all that we need in order to live with him in peace forever.

A time of silence may be kept.

Prayer: An abridged version of the fourth-century prayer of Ephraem:

What shall I give you, Lord, in return for all this kindness?
I shall give you glory.
Glory to you for your love;
Glory to you for your mercy;
Glory to you for coming to save our souls;
Glory to you for receiving the lash;
Glory to you for enduring mockery;
Glory to you for your crucifixion;
Glory to you for your burial;
Glory to you for your resurrection;
Glory to you that you were taken up into heaven;
Glory to you for forgiving all our sins;
I shall give you glory. I shall give you glory.

Suggested songs: 'Thank you, Jesus, thank you, Jesus' or 'Thank you for saving me'

Drama

Characters: Narrator, senior angel, junior angel (both angels dressed neutrally, without wings or halos).
Narrator: This is an authoritative account of a conversation between two angels at a moment of great crisis in the eternal realms. For obvious reasons I choose not to divulge my sources! *(An alarm siren sounds.)* For the first time since the creation of the world there was a red alert in heaven. Twelve legions of angels were put on immediate standby. For some angels, this meant

that they were venturing outside the eternal glory for the first time. *(Two angels enter.)* The angel whose voice you will hear first is senior in the angelic ranks, and has served at one time as Guardian Angel of the planet Earth. *(The junior angel gazes around in wonder.)* And amongst the massed ranks of angels teeming through the glory gate like blazing rainbowed lightning, we should be able to pick out the junior who has been assigned to him as an assistant...
Senior: And this is the cosmos.
Junior: *(gasping)* Why, it's... magnificent... look - billions of suns. Oh... one vast, star-spangled glory. Wheeling galaxies, black space, clouds of creation energy. It's beautiful. I can see the Creator's signature on all of it. It's pulsing with light and glory and...
Senior: So you like moving faster than the speed of light, eh? Did you know you were made to move like this?
Junior: No.
Senior: In fact, the inhabitants of the planet, which we are heading for, paint us with great monster wings.
Junior: You mean... like birds?
Senior: Ha! Yes! They do it to show that we have mastery over time and space.
Junior: You said you knew where we were going!
Senior: Yes. You see that vast spiral? *(Points.)* Well on the edge of it there is one quite ordinary star that has several planets moving around it.
Junior: Which one are we heading for?
Senior: It's called Earth. That's where we are to stand by. Can you see?
Junior: Why, it's quite beautiful. It has glittering oceans and a halo atmosphere. Rugged land masses, and so many animal forms. And humans too. There are deserts and debris, mountains and jungles. Cities. It's wonderful... it's...
Narrator: *(interrupting)* The legions of angels stopped and waited in space, deeply impressive in the power they commanded, close to one spot on earth, invisible to earth's dwellers. An air of sadness came

over them all.
Senior: Shush now. Just watch.
Junior: *(whispering)* But look who it is - it's him! He before whom all heaven falls in adoration. Him! There, thronged by angry, hateful people, jeering and spitting and cursing him. Why doesn't he call us to swoop down and smash them? And... what's he dragging on his shoulders?
Senior: It is called a cross. On it bad men are put to death.
Junior: But they can't do that!
Senior: Shush! He is doing something that no one but he and the blessed Creator understand. Even I have not been allowed to know why he is allowing them to treat him so.
Junior: But you can't mean that they are about to kill him?
Senior: Unless he calls for us. Then it would end in an instant.
Junior: *(Pauses, then murmurs as though urging telepathically.)* Call for us. Call for us.
Senior: He seems bent on entering the only place he's never been before: that dark hole known only to those who flout the Creator's will - those who choose to be cut off from God.
Junior: Does he know that we are here?
Senior: He knows. But I don't think he will call us. I think he will go through it alone.
Junior: But why should... uh... look... they are stretching him over the cross and banging spikes into wrist and ankles... no... no... look what they've done to him.
Senior: *(fighting tears)* Forgive me, I've never wept before. Not since... But wait! What is he saying? A message to those nearby. And to his Father. *(Pause.)* He is taking the battle into the enemy camp.
Junior: I don't understand any of this. Surely...
Senior: Shush! He is doing what Satan would never have dreamed. He is accepting all that hatred, that rebellion. The darkness is wrapping around him. He is driving into it. Headlong! Helpless! Can you hear all

(continued on page 51)

easter easter sunday

only piece that will fit satisfactorily.) In each case, the theory does not fit:

Stolen. The disciples stole the body. Surely not, as they would have had to find enough courage and weapons to fight off a detachment of soldiers (Matthew 27:65,66).

Visions. The disciples only had visions or dreams that they were seeing Jesus. Surely not, because Jesus was able to eat, speak and breathe on them (John 20: 22).

Stories. They made up a story about Jesus appearing to them in the subsequent years. Surely not, because most of the disciples died defending this 'story'. Would they have died for a lie? In any case, surely they would have come up with a better story than the confused ones in the Bible.

Jesus is risen. Only one piece fits! It is the piece which says 'Jesus risen'. The fact is that Jesus had conquered death once and for all on that glorious day. He was and is really alive. That makes all the difference, because it means that we will live for ever with him as well. What wonderful news!

Ideas for music

Choose songs and hymns on the theme of the resurrection. Examples:
'Christ is risen'
'Jesus Christ is risen today'
'Jesus Christ is alive today'
'Well I hear they're singing in the streets'
'The women went to Jesus' tomb'
('Roll the stone away')
'All heaven declares'
'He has risen'
'He is Lord'
'Lord, I lift your name on high'
'Led like a lamb to the slaughter'
'Thine/yours be the glory'

Prayers
Confession and intercession
Ask Jesus' forgiveness for times when we doubt him, ignore him, or behave as if he meant nothing to us. Pray for rest and happiness for those on holiday.
Pray for all who understand what the disciples felt after Jesus' death

---

OUTLINE 19

SERVICE THEME
Can you believe that a dead man rose?

CHURCH YEAR
Easter Sunday

BIBLE BASE
John 20:1-23

ALL-AGE SERVICE SUMMARY
Alternative theories of what happened on the first Sunday are explored, but the only theory that fits the facts is that Jesus had risen from the dead.

THIS WEEK'S RESOURCES
Select the ideas which suit your church tradition and congregation. If there are likely to be many children, make sure that the idea 'Out with joy' is included even if it needs to be modified (a balloon shape on coloured paper would be an alternative).

Setting the scene
Buy an Easter egg in colourful packaging. Before the service, carefully undo the wrapping, remove the chocolate, and reconstruct the package. Hide it in the room where adults and children will worship together.

Invite all the children under a certain age to hunt for something you have hidden. As a clue, tell them it is something that everybody associates with Easter. When the egg has been found, and the children have retaken their seats, open it with great excitement - only to discover that it is empty. Compare this disappointment with the shock that Mary and Peter must have felt on first discovering that the tomb in which Jesus had been laid was empty. They thought that the authorities, who had been cruel to him in life, had been even more callous in death. What they did not realise was that something had happened overnight which was to change their disappointment to joy completely and for ever. That is what we will all celebrate this Easter Day. Turn the disappointment of the empty egg-box into joy by giving everyone a tiny foil covered chocolate egg to eat.

Bible reading
John 20:1-23
Make the most of the excited joy in this reading by asking two readers to read it with an ear to the drama. For

instance, have a female voice read vs 1,2 and 11-18 and a male voice read vs 3-10 and 19-23. They should read as though they were Mary and Peter, almost interrupting each other as they try to tell the story for the first time from their own point of view.

Bible teaching for all ages
During the talk, build up the visual aid on page 51 which shows a broken egg. An overhead projector could be used, the acetates carefully cut along the bold lines. However, it might be more effective in this instance to have the pieces of what is more or less a jigsaw enlarged onto card and presented on a huge board.

The three pictures around the outside show the evidence in John 20:1-23 of the first Easter. Add them one at a time as you explain that:
1 The tomb was empty when Peter and the others found it (vs 3-7).
2 Many people, including Mary, saw Jesus unmistakably alive that day (vs 14-16).
3 The disciples who had been distraught and terrified at Jesus' death were transformed into people bubbling with courage and joy (v 20).

What could account for this evidence? Suggestions have been made! As you comment on them, try to fit the words 'Stolen', 'Visions' and 'Stories' on pieces of egg which don't fit the hole. (The illustration shows the egg complete, with the

Jesus
risen

because they are lonely, in pain or a friend has died.

Pray that everyone who is full of joy in church this Easter may take the reality of the living Jesus with them into their homes, schools or places of work. May others see the difference that trusting in the risen Jesus makes.

Responding in praise

People say that God is dead,
Let us praise the risen Lord.
We know we can shout instead,
Let us praise the risen Lord.
Mary looked inside the tomb,
Let us praise the risen Lord.
Left confused and full of gloom,
Let us praise the risen Lord.

Jesus came to her to say,
Let us praise the risen Lord.
'I'm alive! It's Easter Day!'
Let us praise the risen Lord.
All the facts reveal it's true,
Let us praise the risen Lord.
I believe it. What about you?
Let us praise the risen Lord.

Closing words

Risen Lord Jesus,
Roll away the stone of our doubts;
Let us trust you.
Roll away the stone of our reserve;
Let us proclaim you.
Roll away the stone of our heaviness of heart;
Let us rejoice in you.
Roll away the stone of our fear;

Let us find hope in you,
Now and through all eternity. Amen.

Out with joy

Give each child in church (and any adults who want one) a balloon on which is written the words 'Jesus is alive'. (Children could gather in a group at the front of the church to decorate these with adhesive shapes at an earlier point in the service, while others sing hymns of praise.) Send everyone out at the end of the service waving their balloons joyfully to announce the good news in the surrounding streets.

(continued from page 49)
that shrieking? The demons think they have defeated God.

Junior: This is terrible. Look, the whole area is like night. He's leaving them. He's dying. The Creator of life is dying… like a creature. I can't just wait here. The enemy is winning. We're not lifting a finger to help.

Senior: He has not sent for us. Be still! Wait! He has entered the darkest hole in the universe.

Junior: What do you mean?

Senior: He is in the place of God-forsakenness. The only place the Creator has never been before. The very cell of separation. It is only known to those who revolt against God.

Junior: He's trying to say something. Gasping! What is it he's choking to say?

Narrator: And that is when Jesus shouted in a loud voice, 'It is accomplished!'

Senior: He's done it. He's broken the power. He has won!

Junior: But… but… I don't follow you.

Senior: Listen to that last whisper: 'Father, into your hands I commit my spirit.'

Junior: Is it all over?

Senior: It's just beginning, just beginning… but we are being recalled. I am to stay on standby for a further two days. But you… you must go.

Junior: I'm fearful.

Senior: Don't be. He cannot remain dead. The enemy has done his worst. Now stand by in awe at what the Creator does.

Junior: What a way to treat a king… let alone the King of heaven.

Senior: Time to go… Go on!

Narrator: And in a silent flash of glory the legions of angels were gone. And they left just one. Just one to watch through the dark night of Jesus' death. Just one waiting for the Sabbath to be over. Just one waiting… ready to roll back the stone. *(Exit junior angel.)*

easter sunday

Opening

Ask twelve people (of a variety of ages, semi-rehearsed) to begin the service with a procession. Sombre music should play as they process through the congregation each carrying a board, A3 size, covered with a piece of dark paper or fabric. When they reach the front, they should spread out in a line. Suddenly, perhaps with a clash of cymbals, the music changes to exultant music. They rip the dark shrouds off the boards to reveal the words 'Jesus is alive' in dazzling coloured letters (perhaps cut out of vivid wrapping paper pasted on to white card). They make their way back through the congregation, whooping or shouting 'Alleluia' as they go.

What a context in which to announce the first hymn!

Setting the scene

There is a loud knocking at the door. Stop the service to find out what it is, and ask for the door to be opened. It is a young woman. She is carrying a basket in which are sweet-smelling spices. She walks to the front of the building and this exchange takes place:

Leader: What are you looking for?
Young woman: I am looking for Jesus Christ.
Leader: His body is not here.
Young woman: Why is it not here?
Leader: He is risen indeed! Alleluia!

Explain that this is a truth that makes all the difference in the world. The story we are going to hear today may remind the congregation of what they have just seen and smelled, which is based on an old Russian Orthodox custom. Repeat the leader's last two lines several times during the service.

Bible reading
John 20:11–18
This could be read as a conversation between Mary and Jesus with a narrator reading all the other words.

Bible teaching for all ages

For this talk, everyone in the congregation (both adults and children) needs to be able to see the 'spot the difference' puzzle shown on page 53. Ideally, this should be distributed so that every cluster of three or four people has a copy to gather around and look at. However, in small buildings, showing the pictures on an OHP would be a suitable alternative. Giving out copies as people arrive at the start of a service is convenient, but it is asking a lot of people to expect them to refrain from doing the puzzle before they are instructed to do so! It is preferable to have stewards primed to distribute them as the talk begins.

Pose the question, 'What difference does it make that Jesus has risen from the dead?' To answer, think about the difference it made to Mary on the first Easter morning - the difference between what she expected (the first picture) and what she actually found (the second). At this point, ask the congregation to cluster together and find as many differences as they can. (There are twelve). Depending on the length and informality of the service, you may like to have the answers called out.

Go on to ask, 'What difference does it make to us?' There are, of course, many possible answers, but mentioning three may be most suitable for today's service. (References are to John 20:11-18.)

There's more to life than life!
Christians know that death is not the end. Knowing that meant Mary did not want to cry any more (v 13). That puts everything we do in a new context - even bad things that happen to us are in a new light because we know that one day all will be put right.

We will live with Jesus for ever
Because he has gone to be with God in heaven, we can be sure that we will be there too (v 17). Jesus has done everything we need to take us there - and he is waiting eagerly for us!

A reason to enjoy being alive
Mary had a new task to fulfil, a new purpose in life (v 18). Because Jesus is alive now, there is more to life than eating and sleeping and just getting through. Everything we do he knows about, cares about, and goes through with us. We will never be alone again.

Ideas for music
Choose songs and hymns of joy with an Easter theme.
Examples:
'Children join the celebration'
'Christ is risen, alleluia'
'Here he comes, robed in majesty'
'Jesus Christ is risen today'
'For this purpose'
'Well I hear they're singing in the streets'
'Led like a lamb'
'Thine/yours be the glory'

Prayer
Instead of singing this famous hymn, say it as a spoken, responsive prayer:

Jesus Christ is risen today,
Alleluia!
Our triumphant holy day,
Alleluia!
Who did once upon the cross,
Alleluia!
Suffer to redeem our loss,
Alleluia!
Hymns of praise then let us sing,
Alleluia!
Unto Christ, our heavenly king,
Alleluia!
Who endured the cross and grave,
Alleluia!
Sinners to redeem and save,
Alleluia!

But the pains which he endured,
Alleluia!
Our salvation has procured,
Alleluia!
Now above the skies he's king,
Alleluia!
Where the angels ever sing,
Alleluia!

OUTLINE 20

SERVICE THEME
Why are you crying?

CHURCH YEAR
Easter Sunday

BIBLE BASE
John 20:11–18

ALL-AGE SERVICE SUMMARY
The Easter message is that the resurrection changes our sorrow into joy and makes a huge difference to our lives here and now, and forever.

THIS WEEK'S RESOURCES
There are several items that need to be organised or rehearsed in advance with other people. Where this is not possible, an alternative would be to describe the action as if you had experienced it on another occasion.

easter sunday

Setting the scene

Welcome the congregation and read Psalm 34:1-3. Sing a familiar Easter hymn, such as 'Jesus Christ is risen today'. Point out to those who are too young to read that they can join in by singing 'Alleluia' at the end of each line.

Bible reading
Matthew 28:1-10

Engage the congregation in the reading of the passage. They could help to make the noise of an earthquake (v 2) - practise this before the reading and show them the signal to stop after a couple of seconds. Half of the congregation could read out the words of the angels, the other half saying the words of Jesus. (Both of these could be written up on an overhead projector, printed on to sheets of paper or read from pew Bibles.)

Bible teaching for all ages

Present a very large visual aid of the tomb as shown in the first illustration (page 55). It should be drawn on card, with the 'stone' made from a separate piece of circular card attached with *Blu-tack*. Describe to the congregation the feelings of the women during the three days from Good Friday to Easter Sunday. (At each stage, stop and draw with a thick felt-marker on the stone of the tomb, so that a miserable face appears stage by stage. When you relate the part of the story in which the women meet Jesus, 'roll' the stone through 180 degrees so that the sad face turns into a joyful one.)

1 Describe what the women saw as Jesus died on the cross (Matthew 27:35-38,45,46, 55,56).
2 Talk about the sadness they felt as they saw the body of Jesus placed in a tomb and the stone rolled across the entrance (Matthew 27:57-61).
3 Explain why they went to the tomb on the Sunday morning with spices to embalm the body. Talk about their tears at the thought of never seeing Jesus again, then their fright as the earth shook and an angel appeared (Matthew 28:1-4). As the stone was rolled away, they could barely understand what was going on. They ran to explain what they had seen to the disciples and their fear was completely transformed into joy when they met Jesus and realised that he was alive (Matthew 28:5-9).

We too can share the joy that comes from knowing that Jesus is alive with his Father in heaven, because it means that one day we will see him and live with him forever. Let us take the words of Jesus and the angels as if they were addressed to us: 'Remember what I have told you ... go and tell!' (Matthew 28:7,10).

Ideas for music

Choose songs and hymns of joy for the Easter season.
Examples:
'Jesus Christ is risen today'
'Majesty'
'Celebrate Jesus, celebrate'
'We'll walk the land'
'You are the King of glory'
'King of kings and Lord of lords'
'Shout for joy'
'Led like a lamb'

Statement of belief

Teach the congregation this 'action' statement which they should say and do together:
Christ has died *(stretch arms wide)*,
Christ is risen *(hold open hands open in front of you at chest level)*,
Christ will come again *(lift arms above head and point upwards)*.
Having learnt it, invite the congregation to say it after each line:
Leader: We believe in God the Father, who created our world and sent Jesus to save it. We declare...
Leader: We believe in Jesus, God's only Son, who walked in our world, human but perfect in every way. We declare...
Leader: We believe in the Holy Spirit, whom God sent to live in his people when Jesus returned to heaven. We declare...
Leader: This is the faith of the Christian church. We declare...

Prayers

Confession

Because Jesus has risen to life, sin has lost its power to keep us away from God. So let us tell God we are sorry for our sins, in the certainty that he will forgive us and welcome us as his friends. Because Jesus has risen...
Forgive us, we pray.

Let us confess the wrong things we have done. Because Jesus has risen...
Forgive us, we pray.

Let us confess the wrong things we have said. Because Jesus has risen...
Forgive us, we pray.

Let us confess the wrong things we have thought. Because Jesus has risen...
Forgive us, we pray.

Intercessions

Pray for those who have never heard that Jesus is alive, or have never realised how important that news is.
Pray for those who are trying to help us all tell others about the risen Lord Jesus.
Pray for those who today are sharing the sadness of the women that Easter morning, because they are ill, depressed, lonely or bereaved.
Pray for the victims of war, famine or catastrophe, particularly any who have recently been featured in the news.
After each prayer, the following response could be used:
Give them your peace, Lord,
And show us how to help them.

pentecost

pentecost

OUTLINE 22

SERVICE THEME
God's Spirit at work like fire

CHURCH YEAR
Pentecost

BIBLE BASE
Acts 2:1-4

ALL-AGE SERVICE SUMMARY
With the symbol of fire in mind, the congregation is invited to think of the Holy Spirit as someone who can purify, provide light to life's path and set us on fire for God.

THIS WEEK'S RESOURCES
Some preparation and planning needs to be done if using the visual response in the Bible teaching section, but this will be well worth the trouble as a striking reminder of the prayers of thanks people have said. Choose other items according to the needs of your congregation.

Setting the scene
Light a candle and upturn a glass jar over it. Ask some children what they expect to happen. The flame cannot go on burning because it uses up the oxygen it needs to keep it alight. In the same way, Christians could not keep following Christ if it were not for the Holy Spirit. As we need oxygen, we need the Spirit, even though we cannot see him. Read Romans 8:9-11. Today we will hear ways in which the Holy Spirit is also like a flame that cannot be put out.

Procession
Towards the beginning of the service, play a piece of music that reflects an aspect of the Spirit, such as 'Veni, Sancte Spiritus' from *Laudate, Music of Taize* or a well-known hymn about the Spirit (instrumental only). During this, an adult should place a globe on a table at the front of the room. A procession of children, young people and adults then each bring a lighted candle and place it on the table, completely surrounding the globe with flames of light.

Bible reading
Acts 2:1-4
The congregation can make sound effects as the reading proceeds (the reader should stop after the key words to allow space for this): after 'wind blowing' everyone makes a noise like the wind; after 'tongues of fire' they can flap sheets of paper;

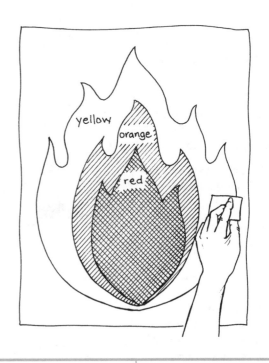

after 'other languages' they should all say, 'Praise the Lord' in any language they know, including the Hebrew 'Alleluia'.

Bible teaching for all ages
At the beginning of the talk, give everyone a pencil and a rectangle of paper, either red, yellow or orange, about 5 cm x 10 cm.
Talk about the coming of the Spirit at Pentecost and pose the question: 'Why a flame?' Suggest three things that a flame tells us about what the Holy Spirit can do.

1 The Spirit can burn away the rubbish in our lives, making us more like Jesus.
2 The Spirit can light up a good path through life for us, showing us what is right to do.
3 The Spirit can set us on fire for God if we ask him to fill us. If we don't, he will just remain in a little 'religious' corner of our lives.

Ask the congregation to respond to this by writing a sentence of praise that they want the Holy Spirit to communicate to God the Father; if they are too young to write, they pentec

ntecost

should draw some things they want to thank God for; if they are too young to draw, they should do some doodles and squiggles for God (he will understand that they are meant as praise - that is what the Holy Spirit does for us).

After a couple of minutes doing this, ask the children to help you collect the papers from the congregation and bring them to the front. Give them pieces of *Blu-tack* and ask them to put the adhesive on the back, then to attach them to a large white board in the flame shaped pattern shown in the diagram (page 56). (To organise this, ask the leaders of the children's groups to assist you at this point. The adult congregation should take the opportunity to sing the much-loved Pentecost hymns which are beyond the children's understanding.)

When the huge flame of praise is complete, send the children back to their seats and comment on some of the contributions that have caught your eye. Invite everyone to come after the service to look more closely at what has been written and drawn.

Ideas for music

Choose songs and hymns about the Holy Spirit at work in our lives. Examples:
'Burn holy fire'
'Come Holy Spirit'
'Fire of God, titanic Spirit'
'I will never be the same again'
There's a wind a-blowing'
'Holy Spirit, truth divine'
'Holy Spirit, we welcome you'
'Rejoice, rejoice, Christ is in you'
'Spirit divine attend/inspire our prayers'
'Spirit of God, unseen as the wind'
'Spirit of holiness'

Prayers

Chant

Picture the disciples in the days before Pentecost, and ask the congregation to join in the chant:

O how long will we have to wait?
O how long will we have to pray?
O how long will we have to praise?
Will the Spirit come today?

After Pentecost the chant is changed:

No longer to have to wait.
The Holy Spirit will help us pray.
The Holy Spirit will help us praise.
The Holy Spirit has come today.

Impromptu prayer

Invite the congregation to form clusters of two or three people by turning on their seats. Ask them to talk together about how they would complete the prayer: 'Holy Spirit, come into our lives to...' After a minute or so, ask them to call out their suggestions and make a list of them. The leader should then turn their suggestions into prayer.

Psalm 68

Give young children streamers made from crêpe paper in flame colours - red, orange and yellow - and show them how to shake them. Teach older children to make a noise like wind whistling through the trees. Encourage adults to call out powerfully, 'Come Holy Spirit!' When each group has learnt its part, practise them together in praise of God. Then announce an acclamation of God's power. The worship leader reads Psalm 68:4,28,29,32-35. Each time the word 'power' is used (four in all) the congregation should interrupt with their words, sounds and actions of praise.

pentecost

pentecost

OUTLINE 23

SERVICE THEME
The Holy Spirit - like a dove

CHURCH YEAR
Pentecost

BIBLE BASE
Mark 1:5-13; John 1:32

ALL-AGE SERVICE SUMMARY
The service should enable the congregation to understand more about the work of the Holy Spirit by thinking about some of the biblical symbols, especially the dove, used to describe the Spirit.

THIS WEEK'S RESOURCES
It is not expected that younger children will be able to grasp symbolic meanings to do with the Holy Spirit, but make sure that they are included by providing plenty of action and visual aids.

Setting the scene

Announce with excitement that today is Pentecost, one of the church's three great festivals. Christmas is long gone - and it seems to be more about shopping than the birth of Jesus. Easter is just a memory - and most people connect it with eggs rather than the day Jesus rose. But Pentecost is today - and wonderfully, no one has stolen it away from the Christians! It is all ours! It is the birthday of the church, since it is the day on which we remember the Holy Spirit being given to all Christians everywhere. So let's celebrate!

Make the suggestion that families do something special together as a treat later in the day - something exciting to mark out the fact that this is as big a day in the life of the church as Christmas or Easter.

Pose the question: what does the Holy Spirit look like? (A tricky one!) Announce that you are going to show everyone a picture of what the Spirit looks like. Create a dramatic build-up as you take the picture from its wrapping to reveal... an empty frame. Explain that the Holy Spirit is invisible. He has to be, because that is how God lives within us. The Bible cannot show us what he looks like, and that is why it uses symbols to help us understand the Spirit's nature - which is what we are all learning about today. Ask a different question: what

difference does the Holy Spirit make to you? You have another picture to show, and this time the congregation will really see something! Create an equally dramatic build-up, and this time reveal (preferably in an identical frame) a mirror. Rotate it so that everyone in the congregation gets a glimpse of himself or herself in it. If, as a church, we have allowed the Spirit to work among us, the change will be noticeable in each one of us. He will be making us more like Jesus, for that is what God has given him to us to do. If you have never asked the Holy Spirit to fill you and change you, today is the day! And if you pray that, meaning it, we will all notice a difference!

Bible reading
Mark 1:5-13

During the reading, symbols could be displayed. For instance, to represent John, you could show a leather belt, some honey and a pair of sandals; to represent Jesus, a picture of a dove. These should be displayed at appropriate moments, the reader pausing briefly.

Bible teaching for all ages

Invite four children to join you at the front of the room. Ask them to hold up objects which show us how the Bible symbolises the Holy Spirit. The first has a bowl of water; the second an electric fan (with ribbons

or streamers attached so that the force of the breeze becomes visible); the third a lighted candle; and the fourth a mirror (on which he or she should breathe to make breath 'visible'.

Remind the congregation what the four symbols are - water, wind, fire and breath. Invite them to chat to the two or three people next to them, children and adults together. Suggest that they choose one of the four objects they can see and talk about what it is about it that helps us understand what God does for us. Explain that anybody who prefers to sit quietly and think about it by themselves may do so. Also that adults need to make sure they listen to the children's ideas, as well as children asking the adults what they think.

Give the congregation two to three minutes to talk, then ask them to call out their suggestions - one object at a time. Give the warmest possible encouragement to everyone who makes a suggestion in this do-it-yourself sermon! (You do not need to exhaust every facet of meaning of every object - a couple of helpful suggestions as to what we can learn from each is sufficient.)

When all the symbols have been mentioned, announce that there is one more that you would like the congregation to think about. Show the picture of a dove (or, if you can bring one along, a live bird!). When Jesus received the Holy Spirit, a dove came down from the sky and settled on him, giving him the most wonderful reassurance that God, his loving Father, was pleased with him (Mark 1:10,11).

That is what the Holy Spirit wants to do for us today. We need not be scared of him, for he comes with tenderness. He will set us to work for God - and that work may be just as hard as the work Jesus had to do (v 12) - but he will always reassure us, with all the gentleness of a dove, that God loves us.

Ideas for music

Choose songs and hymns about the work of the Holy Spirit in the world and in Christian lives and which refer to biblical symbols of the Holy Spirit.

Examples:
'Fire of God, titanic Spirit'
'Holy Spirit, we welcome you'
'This is the day'
'When God breathes'
'Breathe on me, breath of God'
'I will never be the same again'
'When the Spirit of the Lord'
'Give me oil/joy in my heart'
'Like a gentle breeze'
'River, wash over me'
'Spirit of the living God'
'Rejoice, rejoice'

Prayers

Opening words of praise
Set for Pentecost in the Western Rite:

The Spirit of the Lord fills the whole world,
Alleluia, alleluia.
In him all things have their being,
Alleluia, alleluia.
Every sound that is uttered, he knows,
Alleluia, alleluia.
Come, Holy Spirit,
Alleluia, alleluia.

Thanksgiving

Ask everyone, adults and children alike, to find out the name of the person sitting next to them. When they have done so, remind them that the person they have just spoken to is someone in whom the Holy Spirit of God can dwell, and that makes him or her a very special person indeed. God knows their names and they have a special part to play in his world, so it is a good thing to thank God for them. Invite everyone to say together: 'Thank you God for *(the name of their neigbour)*. Amen. What a great God who is able to listen to such a confusion of thank yous and hear everyone individually! Point out that the babies too young to speak were missed out, so make sure that a special prayer of thanks is said for them as well.

Responding to God

Depending on the tradition of the church, congregations will find themselves responding in different ways. If it would be natural to the church to enter a time of ministry in which the Spirit is invited to manifest himself as a blessing to the church, have in mind the presence of children and their special need of explanation, supervision and inclusion.

In other settings, a time during which the congregation have the opportunity to open themselves to the reassurance and direction of the Spirit would be appropriate. Quiet music, live or recorded, could create a peaceful atmosphere. While this is happening, children could be invited to the front of the room to light candles (with careful oversight) as symbols of the Spirit bringing light into our lives. This prayer could bring this section to a close:

Father God, we rejoice in your Spirit;
Jesus Christ, fill us with your Spirit;
Holy Spirit, dwell in us with gentleness and love;
And as you lighten up our lives, may we bring light to the world.
Amen.

Come, Holy Spirit
Leader: Spirit of the Holy God, fill this church.
All: Holy Spirit come as a flame.
Leader: Set us on fire with love for you.
All: Holy Spirit come as a wind.
Leader: Sweep through us with your unseen power.
All: Holy Spirit come as water.
Leader: Wash away all that soils our lives.
All: Holy Spirit come as oil.
Leader: Anoint us to work in your service.
All: Holy Spirit come as breath.
Leader: Make us alive with enthusiasm for you.
All: Holy Spirit come as a dove.
Leader: Bring us together in peace with one another.
All: Spirit of the Holy God, fill this church. Amen.

harvest festival

OUTLINE 24

SERVICE THEME
Accepting God's covenant gratefully

CHURCH YEAR
Harvest thanksgiving

BIBLE BASE
Genesis 8:1 - 9:17

ALL-AGE SERVICE SUMMARY
The theme of the service is that since God creates us and provides for us, we should never forget to be thankful to him.

THIS WEEK'S RESOURCES
Choose the items which will help your congregation to understand how the story of Noah is relevant in today's world, especially God's promise of a continuing provision of food.

Setting the scene

Ask one or two people to show and talk about something which they own that helps them remember a special occurrence - a holiday scrapbook, a diary, a certificate or baptism card, etc. In churches where it is possible, point out and talk about memorial plaques which commemorate special occasions in the life of the building - permanent reminders of people and events which might otherwise be forgotten.

It is good to be able to look at something and have it remind us of someone or something special. There are symbols in the church today which help us bring to mind things way back beyond the time when any of us were born or the buildings stood here. Point out any crosses, Communion elements, stained glass or banners which refer to Jesus, and talk about what they help us remember.

Today, we are all going to think about something which helps us recall one of God's greatest promises. It is something we have all seen, but which you can never get tired of seeing. What could it be? Have a guess and later on we will find out if you are right!

Bible reading
Genesis 8; 9:12-17
Use two voices, one for the narrative, the other to speak the words of God.

Bible teaching for all ages

Immediately after the Bible reading, begin to speak: 'So now you know how the story of Noah ends. The humans safely on dry ground! The animals spreading throughout the world, filling it with life again! And a fantastic promise by God. Sowing seed and reaping a harvest would be part of a human life for ever and ever as the seasons roll on endlessly...' At about this point, you should be interrupted by a family pushing a full shopping trolley down the aisle. (You will need to discuss borrowing this with the manager of your local supermarket. Don't just take and return it - look on it as an opportunity to meet someone who has a key influence on the locality.)

Remark that it is obvious where the family has been, and look in the trolley to see what they have got. What a visual aid of seasons and harvests never ceasing! Out of the trolley pull seven items. They should all come from different countries (wherever possible, developing countries) and they should begin with the initial letters RAINBOW. For example, pull out rice from China, apples from Chile, ice-cream from America (I is a tricky letter - you may have to cheat!), nuts from Brazil, beef from Argentina, olives from Israel, watermelon from Jamaica.

What a rainbow of tastes and colours and varieties! What a wonderful world we live in. Praise God!

Let something 'occur' to you! When we see news of famines in distant countries, often the television pictures focus on aid that is going from our country to theirs. You can get the impression that we feed the world. But it isn't so, as the contents of the shopping trolley have just shown us. In fact, the world feeds us!

The question that comes up many times through the news and in other ways is whether we are treating God's world in the way he intends us to. It was the message of the Garden of Eden (see Genesis 2:15-17) and it is the message of Noah's story. Today, we need to ask ourselves whether we are paying a fair price for the goods from other countries which have become so easy for us to enjoy. (If you wish to develop this, you could talk of and encourage 'fair trade' purchases.) In the countries where seed-time and harvest have never ceased, let us continually remember the debt we owe to the countries which serve and feed us. And let the sign of the rainbow help us never to forget to be thankful to the God who has given us so much.

Learn a Bible verse

'The Lord is faithful to his promises.' (Psalm 145:13GNB)

Prepare a chart or overhead projector acetate in which every letter of the verse and the reference is represented by a dash (as if you were playing 'Hangman'). Ask members of the congregation to call out letters, one at a time. Fill in those which are correct, and when an incorrect one is called out, add a line to a drawing of the church building (taking the place of the rather inappropriate gallows!). When the verse has been completed, ask everyone to read it out. Cover or erase two of the words, then ask everyone to say it again. Repeat this until the whole verse is obliterated and the congregation is saying it from memory. Encourage them to recall it during the week - especially at stressful times.

To operate the game efficiently, have with you this aide-memoire of letters that appear in the verse: A(2), D, E(2), F(2), H(3), I(4), L(3), M(2), O(3), P(2), R(2), S(5), T(3), U.

Ideas for music

Choose songs and hymns about God's provision and promises. Examples:
'God of mercy, God of grace'
'Great is thy/your faithfulness'
'Mister Noah built an ark'
'Noah was the only good man'
'To you, O Lord, our hearts we raise'
'O Lord my God'
('How great thou art')
'We plough the fields and scatter'

Movement and dance

Give children (and/or adults) rainbow-coloured streamers (ribbon or crêpe paper) to twirl during lively songs.

Prayers
Responsive prayer of thanks
This prayer will need a little adaptation to local conditions in countries outside the UK:

In the springtime, when new life is seen in the young plant shoots; when leaves and blossoms are rich on the trees; when the sun begins to warm the earth and all is fresh and green; that is when we thank you.
We thank you, Lord, that you remember us.
In the summer, when the days are long and warm, and the fruit and plants are growing to maturity; when all is bright and vibrant; that is when we thank you.
We thank you, Lord, that you remember us.
In the autumn, when the harvest is ready to be gathered, and the berries hold a promise for the future growth; when the days grow shorter and the winds blow; that is when we thank you.
We thank you, Lord, that you remember us.
In the winter months, when all is sleeping, waiting to be stirred to life; when the darker days and colder weather make the memories of summer distant; that is when we thank you.
We thank you, Lord, that you remember us.
We thank you, Lord, that you remember us through all the seasons of the year, and through all the seasons of our lives. Amen.

Rainbow prayers
Ask people to cluster into groups of three or four (as many adults and children as can comfortably chat without moving any furniture). Give each group a piece of paper with the letters RAINBOW written vertically down one side. Ask them to write a seven line prayer of thanks to God, each line beginning with a different letter of the word 'rainbow' (give an option to do this individually). Bring the prayers to the front and pin them on a board which already has a rainbow on it. Read out one or two and encourage people to look at the others after the service. An example is:
'Robots, Applemacs, Internet, Nintendo, BSkyB, Outer space - Wow!

Confession
Based on 1 John 1:9:

Father God, you have promised to hear us when we call to you. Lord, we confess our sins.
Keep your promise and forgive us, we pray.
For the times when we have hurt others through the words we have said, Lord, we confess our sins.
Keep your promise and forgive us, we pray.
For the times when our actions have been harmful and not loving, Lord, we confess our sins.
Keep your promise and forgive us, we pray.
For the times when we have forgotten you and ignored your commands, Lord, we confess our sins.
Keep your promise and forgive us, we pray.
Lord, we know we have sinned and done what is wrong. In your mercy, forgive us, and help us to live for you. Amen.
© Mary Hawes

harvest festival

OUTLINE 25

SERVICE THEME
The wonder of creation

CHURCH YEAR
Harvest thanksgiving

BIBLE BASE
Psalm 148

ALL-AGE SERVICE SUMMARY
All creation brings praises to God, giver and provider.

THIS WEEK'S RESOURCES
This is not a traditional harvest thanksgiving, but looks more widely at God's creation, valuing human work (in its widest sense) and providing an opportunity to praise God in different ways.

Setting the scene

Use 'dingbat' clues (below) to introduce the theme. The first two are for the northern hemisphere and relate to Autumn ('Leaves are falling' and 'Days are getting shorter'. The third is for the southern hemisphere (Spring is in the air).

Before the service, arrange for many people, of varying ages, to bring to church something that represents the work they do. The items could include baby ointment, building materials, an educational toy, some medicine, a student's book, a food product, accountancy papers, and so on. Be sure that the 'work' of pre-school children, carers, home-keepers, artists and charity volunteers is included alongside that of students and paid workers. Invite those who have come prepared to bring forward their symbols and place them on a table at the front of the room. Other people in the congregation may realise that they happen to carry with them objects that represent their work, and they should be encouraged spontaneously to add to the display.

Talk about the variety of what can be seen, perhaps asking some people questions about what they have brought. Comment on how much we would have to stretch our knowledge to know everything about all the kinds of work on display. But God knows all about them! Psalm 148 says that everything worships God, and today we are stretching ourselves in our worship to do the same - not just letting the natural produce of his creation worship him, but allowing the work of the whole created world to give him praise. (It might be possible to incorporate the items collected in a prayer after the psalm has been read.)

Bible reading
Psalm 148:1–14 (GNB)

This could be illustrated with ten images as it is read. If a blackout can be used in the room, the images should be slide transparencies (ask a keen photographer in the congregation if he or she has suitable holiday photographs). Alternatively, images on an overhead projector could be used cumulatively, thus:

Verses 1,2: slide of a clear sky or the bright light of an overhead projector;

verses 3,4: slide of a night scene or children's gummed paper stars scattered on the top part of the OHP image;

verses 5,6: a sunset or a coin added to the OHP to give a sun-shaped silhouette;

verse 7: sea or wave-shaped paper at the foot of the OHP;

verse 9: a landscape or cut-out trees;

verse 10: animals and birds;

verse 11: slides of important people or silhouettes of adults;

verse 12: children;

verses 13,14: people in poses of worship.

Bible teaching for all ages

Psalm 148 says that everything is made for the praise of the Lord. Expand this under four headings, each time illustrating the point in one or more of the ways suggested. The first two headings represent the unknown, the third and fourth, the known. You may prefer to separate the four sections and thus integrate the talk with the rest of worship.

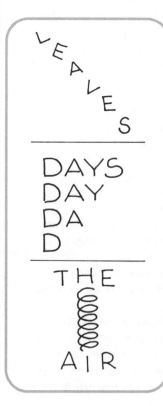

aimonnut | trufi fere | dwil mianla | sterof | cimodest minala

preliet | drib | gink | dol serpon | goynu sernop

Things we don't yet understand (vs 1–6)

Heaven: read part of Revelation 4:2b–11 or sing verse 2 of 'Holy, holy, holy, Lord God Almighty', or show an artist's representation of heaven.

Sun, moon and stars: show a picture or model or talk about our modern understanding of the universe. Though this is quite different from that of the biblical writers, we still do not understand everything about it.

Say these words together, the leader speaking first, then everyone repeating them: 'Things we don't understand, praise the Lord.'

Things which can scare us (vs 7,8)

Monsters: produce something which is harmless in itself yet could be frightening, eg spider in a glass jar with lid on, balloon which could burst.

Wind: discuss other awesome things such as darkness, waves and aspects of the weather. (Distinguish briefly between the things mentioned here which scare us but which are just part of the natural world, and things which, usually as a result of the sinful human nature, are essentially destructive and evil such as injustice, racism, etc which are not glorifying to God.)

Say together: 'Things which scare us, praise the Lord.'

Things we know (vs 9–12)

Show pictures of things mentioned in the psalm (eg mountain, fruit-tree, forest, domestic animal, wild animal, reptile, bird, king, young person, old person) or use the quiz above. Children can participate by identifying the pictures at the same time as adults solve the anagrams. Discuss other things which might praise God by their existence.

Say together: 'Things we know, praise the Lord.'

The worship of God's people (vs 13,14)

Words: show a hymn book, prayer book or something else which literally puts our praise into words.

Work: ask everyone to write a few words describing their work (explain the broad sense in which you are using the word, encompassing the constructive activity that is part of everyone's life) on an adhesive sticker (have pencils available) and fix these to a large piece of paper. Refer to any displays and artwork which draw attention to people's 'work'.

Say together: 'All God's people, praise the Lord.'

Finish with this summary:
Things we don't understand, praise the Lord.
Things which scare us, praise the Lord.
Things we know, praise the Lord.
All God's people, praise the Lord.

Ideas for music

Choose songs and hymns which praise God for creation and his provision.
Examples:
'All things bright and beautiful'
'At harvest time'
'Fill your hearts with joy'
'Who paints the skies into glorious day?'
'Oh Lord my God (How great thou art/you are)'
'We plough the fields and scatter'
'Who put the colours in the rainbow?'

Prayers

Psalm 148

Praise the Lord from up in heaven,
Praise the Lord from all the earth.
Praise him all his angel host,
Praise the Lord from all the earth.
Praise him sun and moon and stars,
Praise the Lord from all the earth.
Praise him monsters in the sea,
Praise the Lord from all the earth.
Clouds and rain and wind and snow,
Praise the Lord from all the earth.
Hills and mountains, trees and crops,
Praise the Lord from all the earth.
Birds and beasts and creeping things,
Praise the Lord from all the earth.
Kings and those who rule the world,
Praise the Lord from all the earth.
Men and women, young and old,
Praise the Lord from all the earth.
Made to praise the Lord's great name,
Praise the Lord from all the earth.

Prayer of commitment

Invite several people of different ages and life-styles to describe their 'work' in one sentence. All respond with the words from Colossians 3:17, continuing in this pattern:

A: I work in Green's factory and one thing I do is pack boxes.
Leader: Everything you do or say should be done in the name of Jesus.
All: Give thanks through him to God the Father.
B: I am a home-maker and one thing I do is cook meals.
Leader: Everything you do or say should be done in the name of Jesus.
All: Give thanks through him to God the Father.
C: I am retired and one thing I do is to look after my grandchildren.
Leader: Everything you do or say should be done in the name of Jesus.
All: Give thanks through him to God the Father.

A creation creed

Leader: We believe in God the Creator
A: who took great care in making our world;
B: who makes each of us in God's image;
All: who wants our help in running the world.
Leader: And we believe in Jesus, the Son
A: who worked with God creating our world;
B: who lived and worked here just as we do;
All: who died to save us and all the world.
Leader: And we believe in God the Spirit,
A: who worked with God creating our world
B: who works here now through all that we do;
All: who fills us with God's creative power.
A and B: We believe that one day all things will come together with Christ as Head.
All: And this is our creation creed.
© Eileen Turner

harvest festival

OUTLINE 26

SERVICE THEME
Thanking God for food and drink

CHURCH YEAR
Harvest thanksgiving

BIBLE BASE
Deuteronomy 8:7-20; Psalm 104:13-15

ALL-AGE SERVICE SUMMARY
Remembering that the abundance and variety of the food and drink we enjoy are a gift from God; he wants us to use the gift wisely, remembering that some people do not have enough.

THIS WEEK'S RESOURCES
Make the most of the opportunity for using aids which are not only visual, but tactile and taste-full! There are suggestions at the end of the outline for ways of extending the harvest theme beyond the all-age service.

Setting the scene

Carry to the centre of the church a large, gift-wrapped box containing packets, tins and bottles of food and drink. Ask for guesses as to what is inside and, once a few suggestions have been made, take out the contents and stack them on a table. Point out that although these products have been bought at a local shop, they are really presents from God, who provides us with all we need. How? It is God who had the brilliant idea of putting seeds inside fruit so that plants will keep on and on growing. It is God who put the excellent idea inside human heads of cooking and arranging fruit and vegetables so that they would be really enjoyable to eat. It is God who made men and women clever enough to organise the processing, transport and sale of these things so that we can buy them in the shops. Today we will all find out about God's part in making something that we need so much, something we enjoy so much! Read Psalm 104:14

Bible reading
Deuteronomy 8:7-11
To explain the context of the reading, say that the people of Israel were about to enter and live in the land that God had promised them. They are hearing what it will be like there and what their responsibilities are for their new life.

Bible teaching for all ages

Using the illustrations on page 65, prepare an overhead projector acetate or large chart which contains pictures of wheat, barley, grapes, pomegranates, olives, and honey. Cover each picture individually. Ask volunteers to call out the foods they remember being mentioned in the Bible reading, and uncover them as correct guesses are made. These words were written just before God took his special people, the Israelites, into the beautiful Promised Land that he had prepared for them to live in. Do you remember what they had to do when they arrived and found the land so good that this food grew plentifully on their farms? Read Deuteronomy 8:10.

Referring again to the pictures, talk of the variety in what God provides, and how enjoyable this makes eating. Produce two bunches of grapes, black and white, and ask children to explain how they differ. Choose some to taste the difference. Then produce a jar of set honey and compare it with runny honey, and look at some breakfast cereals made from the same crop. Aren't we fortunate in this country? God has given us so much abundance to enjoy that we must not take it for granted.

Two-thirds of the world is seriously under-nourished. They are desperately grateful for their food even if it has no variety. Let us respond by using our food wisely - taking care to eat a healthy diet that keeps our bodies fit for God's work, trying not to waste food, willingly sharing with those who are hungry. In these ways we are 'remembering the Lord' as we enjoy the abundance he has given us (Deuteronomy 8:17,18).

Ideas for music

Choose songs and hymns on the theme of harvest which express gratitude for God's provision or touch on our responsibilities to use his gift wisely.
Examples:
'At harvest-time we celebrate'
'Fear not, rejoice and be glad'
'Great is the Lord and most worthy of praise'
'I am the bread of life'
'Now we sing a harvest song'
'We plough the fields and scatter'
'For health and strength and daily food'

Prayers
Thanksgiving
Say the Lord's Prayer together, pointing out that Jesus tells us to pray for our daily bread (our basic necessities) and that God has responded with great abundance. Follow it with this prayer:

Not only, Lord, for daily bread,
But butter, *Marmite*, chocolate spread,
You give us marmalade and jam,

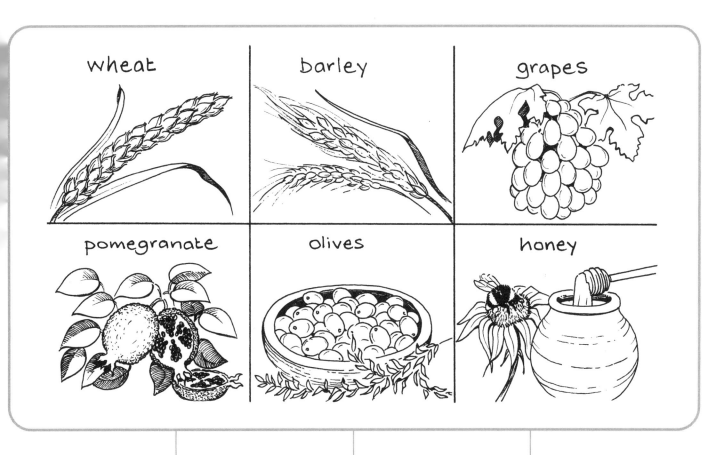

wheat

barley

grapes

pomegranate

olives

honey

Cheese and chutney, pâté, ham.
Help us always, God above,
To thank you for these gifts of love.

Confession
Hold a short interview with someone who has a particular involvement with a relief agency, as a supporter, donor or representative. Ask them to lead prayers of confession and intercession about the needs of the hungry. (These could mention the subjects such as: our careless use of food; our forgetfulness of God's provision; our deafness, satisfied as we are, to the cries of the hungry; a resolution to change.)

Praising God for water
There is one commodity on which we are totally dependent. It makes up 70% of the planet's surface and covers 10% of the land. It makes up 65% of our bodies and we cannot

survive more than four days without it. What is it? It's water! Ask the congregation to turn to those next to them and compile a mental list of the things we need water for (particularly to do with food and drink). After a minute or so, praise God who richly supplies the earth with water, either in a time of open prayer in which children and adults are encouraged to mention one thing on their list, or with the leader summing up the suggestions of the congregation in a single prayer.

Prayer with silences
In the pauses, everyone should think of the foods and drinks which apply to them personally:

Creator God, we thank you for feeding us so well every day. Thank you for the food we ate at breakfast this morning... Bless the farmers who

grew the food we ate.
Thank you for the meal we are looking forward to eating when we get home from church... Bless the person who prepares the food that we will eat.
Thank you for the special food we eat at parties... Thank you for the special people who share that food with us.
Thank you for the food which we have as a favourite treat... Thank you that there is so much food to enjoy that we can treat ourselves like this. For your abundant supplies we give you heartfelt thanks. Amen.

Enjoying food and drink
Make the enjoyment of food and drink an integral part of today's worship in one of these ways:
1 In order to focus minds during a prayer of thanks, pass around something for everyone to eat.

Satsumas broken into segments might be suitable.
2 After the service, provide coffee, tea, cold drinks, crisps and biscuits for everyone to enjoy.
3 Invite the congregation (in advance) to bring picnic lunches to pool and share after the service.
4 Organise a 'feast' one afternoon or evening. It could either be an all-age event or specifically for children. Include in it some kind of activity which involves preparing food or sweets to be eaten later in the event. There could also be games which have edible prizes, and an unusual kind of meal - perhaps one which involves going to different locations for each course.

© Alison Stevenson

bible sunday

bible sund

OUTLINE 27

SERVICE THEME
What's in the Bible?

CHURCH YEAR
Bible Sunday

BIBLE BASE
2 Timothy 3:10–17

ALL-AGE SERVICE SUMMARY
This week's material encourages people to look at the Bible as a resource for living a Christian life today, using as a starting point the kinds of discoveries that can be made in libraries, personal reference books and through information technology.

THIS WEEK'S RESOURCES
Two ideas are given for 'setting the scene'. The first will need much more organisation, though it will be of much more interest and provide a greater amount of interaction.

Setting the scene 1

Beforehand, invite families or different groups (don't be ageist!) to search the Internet, local libraries or their own guidebooks for information about your local area. Ask each group to find some of the following:

• something they didn't know before about their own area;
• something that was difficult to understand or just seemed odd;
• something that is useful to know;
• something which is good news;
• somewhere locally that you can get help.

Explain to the congregation what each group has been doing and ask the groups in turn to tell everyone one each of the items above. Review the different ways in which the groups found answers to questions about their own surroundings. Today is Bible Sunday and we are going to ask how the Bible can help us in our own surroundings and in the place where we live.

Setting the scene 2

To prepare, obtain a local guide book that covers your own area. Use the same topics, making notes of the answers you find. Tell the congregation what you have discovered. Explain that you used a guide book to discover more about the locality and that it is possible to use the Bible in a similar way, to find out more about God and about the Christian life.

Bible reading
2 Timothy 3:10–17

Before the reading, explain the historical situation - that Paul the missionary had been put into prison because his enemies wanted to stop him spreading the good news about Jesus. However, there were still younger Christians, like Timothy, working for God and Paul wrote to give them encouragement and advice. This reading is from the second letter he wrote to Timothy. The point could be emphasised visually by splitting the reading into two sections, one read by an older person who then hands the Bible on to someone younger.

Bible teaching for all ages

To prepare, write out the following items and make enough copies to give one to every group of six to eight people. (Also provide blank paper and crayons for younger children.)

• Something new that someone has recently discovered in the Bible.
• Something that is difficult to understand in the Bible, or which just seems odd.
• Something useful, some special words (perhaps a favourite quote) from the Bible.
• Some good news from the Bible.
• Something that has helped someone when they didn't know where to turn.

Remind the congregation of the questions given to your information explorers. In everyday life, we discover something we didn't know before, almost every day! We often come across situations that we don't understand or which seem odd. We also get excited when we discover something really special and useful. Or it may be that what we discover is so special that we learn the words carefully and they remain with us for the rest of our lives. Sometimes we hear really good news. At other times we need to look for help.

Exploring the Bible

Can we find all these things in the Bible? Ask everyone to form groups of six or seven where they are sitting, with a good mixture of ages where possible. Distribute the prepared sheets of paper and challenge the groups to think of answers to one or two of the items. During this time, ask younger children to draw a picture about a Bible story they know or something they have done recently.

Allow five minutes for this activity and then encourage each group to feed back on one of their items, very briefly. (With a larger congregation it may not be possible for every group to feed back, in which case simply ask a few groups to do so.) Be sure to ask those who have drawn pictures to show them if they wish to.

Afterwards, say that you asked earlier if all these items could be found in the Bible and the answer has to be a resounding 'yes' - and more. In another of Paul's letters to the church in Rome, he wrote that 'the Scriptures were written to teach and encourage us by giving us hope' (Romans 15:4 CEV).

Close by giving a survey of different ways in which people can find out more about the Bible. Show a range of Bible reading notes for different age groups and a small selection of other interesting materials, such as *The Children's Guide to the Bible*, Robert Willoughby, Scripture Union.

Browsing time

It would be ideal to provide a bookstall of Bible-related publications for the congregation to look through after the service. Make sure that someone is available to advise those who may be looking for Bible reading aids, perhaps for the first time.

Bible Sunday drama

An excellent play for two people is available from the Bible Society: 'The Greatest Story Ever Sold', from *Entertaining Angels*, Stephen Deal, Bible Society. Also, *Oh no, not the Nativity!: sketches through the church year* (Scripture Union) contains a sketch specifically written for Bible Sunday.

Ideas for music

Choose songs and hymns about the Bible and how its message brings us good news and hope.
Examples:
'Spirit of God, unseen as the wind'
'Jesus, let me meet you in your word'
('Now in reverence and awe')
'God has spoken by his prophets'
'Jesus restore to us again'
'Lord, you sometimes speak in wonders'
'Lord, your word shall guide us/thy word abideth'
'Open this book that we may see your word'

Prayers

A prayer of welcome

Adapted from Psalm 119:97-106, this prayer encourages us to welcome God's teaching into our lives:

Your word is a lamp that gives light wherever we walk.
Lord, teach me your ways.
Nothing is completely perfect, except your teachings.
Lord, teach me your ways.
Your laws never leave our lives; they make us wiser than our enemies.
Lord, teach me your ways.
Obeying your word makes us wiser.
Lord, teach me your ways.
We obey your word instead of following a way that leads to trouble.
Lord, teach me your ways.
Your teachings are sweeter than honey.
Lord, teach me your ways.
Your word is a lamp that gives light wherever we walk.
Lord, teach me your ways.

Bible harvest

In many countries of the world it would be a luxury for Christians to own a whole Bible of their own and yet it is likely that every household in the congregation has at least one. Many will have more than one. Ask the congregations to huddle into clusters where they sit and try to add up how many Bibles (including books containing just the New Testament and Psalms) are owned by the people in each cluster. When each group has a tally, find out which group has the most Bibles!

Say that it is good to know that the Bible is so important to them as a congregation, but challenge them to see whether they could spare just one or two to help others read and study God's word. Bibles in English can be used almost anywhere in the world by agencies such as (in the UK) Book Aid (Tel: 020 8857 7794). A collection of Bibles in good condition could be made over the next few weeks. Conclude by praying for those who struggle to study, preach and teach because they have limited access to the Bible.

God's creation

God's creation

OUTLINE 28

CHRISTIAN THEME
God's creation

SERVICE THEME
'I created you'

BIBLE BASE
Genesis 1:1 – 2:25; Psalm 8:3–5; Ephesians 1:4–10

ALL-AGE SERVICE SUMMARY
Considering what it means to be made in God's image and celebrating the wonder of our world.

THIS WEEK'S RESOURCES
Some large-scale visuals are required for this service. If this is impractical, they could be transferred onto overhead projector acetates, but this will lose some of the impact and enjoyment, especially for children.

Setting the scene

Present a huge piece of paper on one wall of the room. On it are already drawn a sun and a moon. Invite any who are old enough to grasp a pen but too young to read to go to it with a grown-up. They are each to draw a star on the picture of the sky. Meanwhile, those who are older sing a hymn. Thank the children for their contribution to your worship, and ask them to listen out for what they have drawn during the response, based on Psalm 8 (see below).

Bible reading

Genesis 1:26–31
Briefly recount the story from Genesis 1, the creation of the world, before beginning to read from verse 26.

Read Ephesians 1:4–10
If possible, display a picture of the earth taken from space during this reading.

Bible teaching for all ages

Invite the congregation to form groups of six to nine people (no bigger), adults and children together. Each group needs paper and a pencil. It will help them to have a Bible open at Genesis chapter 1.

Ask one person from each group to come to the front - neither the oldest nor the youngest. You will whisper to them one of the things that God created. They must return to the group and draw it. The person who guesses what it is comes to the front to be told the next object to be drawn, and so on.

The first drawing is of the sun; subsequently tell the representatives to draw birds, fruit trees, women, wild animals, men, fish, the moon. When about two-thirds of the groups have finished, stop the game and say a prayer of thanks for all that God made.

Explain that the world was very good before human beings were made, but they added something special to it. Sometimes we pretend that animals and plants are like humans in the way they think and behave. That is all right in stories, but it is not really true, because God said something special about human beings. He said, 'I will make them to be like me.'

What does that mean? Show a large visual aid (prepared beforehand) consisting of the outline of a human. (An easy way to prepare this is to have someone lie on the paper and draw around him or her. Cut the outline into four pieces with the words in bold (points 2 to 5 below) written in large letters. You will also need one extra piece that does not fit anywhere in the outline, with the words in point 1. As you explain what it means to be 'in the image of God', fit the pieces into the outline.

Reject the first piece because it does not fit, but note how wonderful it is that the others are true.

1 *God looks like a huge person.* No!
2 *Humans know the difference between being good and being bad.* Yes!
3 *Humans can be creative and artistic.* Yes!
4 *Humans are spiritual and can be friends of God.* Yes!
5 *Humans can live forever with God.* Yes!

Ideas for music

Choose songs and hymns about our relationship with God and the value he sets on us as human beings.
Examples:

'All people that on earth do dwell'
'I'm special'
'Come rejoice before your maker'
'He gave me eyes'
'Jesus, Lord of everything'
'He has clothed us with his righteousness'
'I am fearfully and wonderfully made'
'The earth is the Lord's'
'The King is among us'
'There are hundreds of sparrows'
'We are chosen'
'There are lots of ways that I can praise'

Prayers

Based on Psalm 8

Leader: O Lord, our Lord, your greatness is seen in all the world!

Adults: Your praise reaches up to the heavens;

Children: It is sung by children and babies.

Leader: You are safe and secure from your enemies;

Adults: You stop anyone who opposes you.

Children: I look at the sky, which you have made,

Leader: And at the moon and stars, which you have set in their place.

Adults: Then I ask myself, what is it about humans, that makes you even think of them?

Children: What is it about children that makes you love them?

Leader: Yet you made us inferior only to yourself; you crowned humankind with glory and honour.

Adults: You appointed us as rulers over everything you made;

Children: You made us the best of all the things you made.

Rhyme for young children

I can hear and I can see,
Thank you, God, for making me.
(Cup ears and point to eyes.)
I am strong and I am free,
Thank you, God, for making me.
(Flex muscles and fling arms wide.)
You have made the earth and sea,
Thank you God for making me.
(Draw a circle in the air, then make waves.)
Thank you, God, for making me.
(Stretch up tall.)

creation

God's creation

creation
creatio

OUTLINE 29

SERVICE THEME
'I am putting you in charge'

CHRISTIAN THEME
God's creation

BIBLE BASE
Genesis 1:26–30; 2:15; Psalm
8:6–8; Romans 8:19–23

ALL-AGE SERVICE SUMMARY
Considering how people have
carried out God's charge to rule
all he has made.

THIS WEEK'S RESOURCES
This service follows on well from
the subject of the previous
outline 'I created you'. Choose
items to suit your congregation,
but try to keep a good balance
between listening and doing.

Setting the scene

Show some useful objects which
God has given us through the
cleverness of human beings.
Comment: 'Hasn't God made
humans wonderfully ingenious!' as
you mention, for example, dental
floss, hair gel, contact lenses,
synchromesh gear boxes, *Cling film*,
ring pull cans, sticky tape.

Invite the congregation to cluster
into groups, to think of other things
they use which show the cleverness
of humankind in using God's
resources. In a time of prayer, invite
them to shout out, 'Thank you, God,
for...' from anywhere in the room, not
worrying if someone else speaks at
the same time.

After two minutes, go on to ask
the groups to think of things that
remind them of the foolishness of
humans in using God's resources, eg
acid rain, graffiti, land mines. When
they have spoken to each other,
explain that this foolishness is
today's subject.

Bible reading

Genesis 1:26–30; 2:15
Show pictures of people (adults and
children) from different ethnic
backgrounds and of natural scenes
or cultivated crops during this
reading. Colour photographs can be
effectively transferred on to special
overhead projector acetates at
specialist shops.
Romans 8:19–23
Leave a picture of a natural scene

displayed during this reading.

Bible teaching for all ages

One way in which people are like
God is that they themselves can be
creative. Illustrate this ingenuity by
asking people to call out things
which can be made from some of
the following: milk, water, salt, sugar,
flour, egg. (Answers will include
things like sauce, biscuits, scones,
souffle, egg flip, meringues,
pancakes, paste, playdough.) Give
examples of other uses of our
creative gifts.

People have done remarkable
things with God's raw materials.
Sometimes we make creation better
(plants grow better with nutrients
and in greenhouses and we've even
invented new foods like nectarines).
But we have done some terrible
things as well. Read Genesis 1:28
and 2:15, then give examples of how
humans have failed God by abusing
Earth's resources on a world-wide
scale.

It is no good blaming someone
else, for we all contribute to this in
little ways. Give out photocopies of
the composite picture on page 71
and ask the congregation to form
groups and identify ways in which
people are failing to use their
position 'in charge of the world' in a
godly way.

After a few minutes, regain
attention and point out that we hear
a lot these days about being 'green'.

God has appointed us rulers over all
creation (Psalm 8:6). He will one day
ask us to account for how we've
carried out that appointment.

Quiz

Display the word CREATION.
Announce that all the answers to
the following questions use some of
the letters from the word in a
different order.
1 Water which falls on the earth.
(Rain.)
2 Clean animal, usually a pet. *(Cat.)*
3 A dirty animal, sometimes
spreading disease. *(Rat.)*
4 Metal found in the earth. *(Iron, tin.)*
5 Mountain. *(Tor.)*
6 Bird. *(Crane.)*
7 What we breathe and birds fly in.
(Air.)
8 What God expected people to do
with the food. *(Eat.)*
9 What God expected people to do
with the world. *(Care.)*
10 Something people have made
with God's raw materials. *(Can, car,
cot, net, train, etc.)*

Action song

Ask a group of adults and children
to sing this together, with ten people
holding up appropriate items and an
explanation, if necessary.

Ten green Christians sitting on
the fence,
Ten green Christians sitting on
the fence,
And if one green Christian would go

o more expense,
Display a biodegradable cleaning
product.)
here'd be nine green Christians
itting on the fence.

line... stop the negligence.
A mock drum of toxic waste.)
ight... some campaign commence.
A placard on an environmental
ssue.)
even... fight the ignorance.
Can of unleaded petrol.)
ix... use their influence.
Letter to MP.)
ive... use intelligence.
Bottles and paper for recycling.)
our... follow their conscience.
Fairly traded goods.)
hree... took inconvenience.
Recycled toilet paper.)
wo... stop extravagance.
'More with less' or vegetarian
cookbook.)
One... show some penitence.
Drops to knees.)
Just one green Christian can make a
difference!

Ideas for music

Choose songs and hymns about
human responsibility for the created
world or about God's wonderful gift
to us of the natural world.
Examples:
'For the beauty of the world'
'God in his love for us'
'I have seen the golden sunshine'
'O Lord my God, when I in awesome
wonder'
'Our God is one who makes things'
'Praise to the Lord, the Almighty'
'Stand up, clap hands'
'Think of a world without any flowers'

Prayers

Praise and draw

Read Psalm 8:6-8. Children are given
felt markers and invited to come to
the wall picture (see the 'Setting the
scene' activity in the previous outline
'I created you'), adding creatures
mentioned in the verses. Meanwhile
the rest of the congregation sings
another hymn expressing awe at
God's creation.

Noisy praise

Respond to Psalm 8 with a prayer
that continues this pattern:
Leader: The sheep praise you by
saying:
All: Baa! O Lord, our Lord, your
greatness is seen in all the world!
Leader: The sea praises you by
saying:
All: Whoosh! O Lord, our Lord, your
greatness is seen in all the world!

Confession

Let us say sorry for the way people
have spoilt what God created:
For the pollution we cause by
throwing rubbish on the land,
sewage and chemicals in our water,
and harmful gasses into the
atmosphere. Father we are sorry we
have spoiled your world;
Forgive us and help us.

For the changes in our climate that
have come about because of our
lifestyle: the holes in the ozone layer,
the growth of deserts, the flooding
due to deforestation. Father we are

sorry we have spoiled your world;
Forgive us and help us.

For the greed which makes some
countries take more than their fair
share of food and resources. Father
we are sorry we have spoiled your
world;
Forgive us and help us.

For the irresponsibility and political
intrigue which often prevents
anything being done about these
issues. Father, we are sorry we have
spoiled your world;
Forgive us and help us.

For the fact that it is always the
poor who suffer most. Father, we are
sorry we have spoiled your world;
Forgive us and help us.

worship

worshipping God

SERVICE THEME
How can we praise and
worship God?

CHRISTIAN THEME
Worship

BIBLE BASE
2 Samuel 6:12–22; 7:1–29

ALL-AGE SERVICE SUMMARY
Using the story of David, the
material challenges the
congregation to view worship in
a wider context.

THIS WEEK'S RESOURCES
It is important, given the theme
of the service, to choose items
which will challenge the
congregation to try something
new or different, rather than
selecting those which feel safe!

iuMcs   sueeQitns   reraPy

esnfOfrig   agtEin   eacnD

Setting the scene
Distribute six large envelopes to
members of the congregation and
invite them to stand at the front of
the room. Each envelope bears one
letter (written very large) which
together make up the word PRAISE,
and inside each is a piece of paper
bearing the words of a Bible verse
about praising God. One at a time,
invite the six (who should represent
a wide age-range) to open their

envelope and read out the verse.
Comment on each very briefly.
Suggested verses are:
Psalm 92:1; Psalm 95:1; Psalm 96:2;
2 Corinthians 1:3; Philippians 1:11; 1
Peter 1:3.

Bible reading
2 Samuel 6:12–22 (GNB)
This reading could be heard over a
well-known song of praise -
instruments only, but ensure that

this is not played so loudly that the
congregation does not hear the
story. An alternative would be to
hear the music both before and after
the reading.

Bible teaching for
all ages
Remind the congregation of the
story contained in 2 Samuel 6:12–22,
and explain what the Covenant Box
held and why it was so special to the

worshi

sraelites. Why was David anxious that this procession should be exactly right? Because he wanted to honour God (v 21). That and that alone should motivate all our praise. Identify six activities through which David tried to honour God. One by one, display enlarged copies of the six pictures (page 72). Ask the congregation, chatting together in twos and threes, adults and children together, to discover what each is - either by unscrambling the words or identifying the pictures. When they have had time to solve each one, point out where it comes in the story and say a few words about why and how it is appropriate in worshipping God today. The six are: music (6:15); quietness (7:18); prayer (7:27); offerings (6:17); eating (6:19); dance (6:14).

Sum up by saying that there will always be some who are embarrassed by the way other people worship (6:20). However, when we worship God, it is an activity to take part in, not a performance to watch. If we just become spectators like Michal, we may feel awkward about the different ways in which other people worship. We need to come honestly before God and honour him in the best way we can, no matter what that way is. It has to be 'with all our might' (v 14).

Ideas for music
Choose songs and hymns which offer worship to God using several different styles and traditions of music.
Examples:
'God is good, we sing and shout it'
'Let us praise God together'
'Let us praise his name with dancing'
'I will dance, I will sing'
'Well I hear they're singing in the streets'
'Let us with a gladsome (gladly with one) mind'
'O give thanks to the Lord, all you his people'
'Praise to the Lord, the Almighty'
'Worthy, the Lord is worthy'

Prayers
Psalm 24
Psalm 24 suggests a celebration of the arrival of the Covenant Box - the focus of God's presence - in Jerusalem. We can imagine huge, excited crowds on either side of the city gates. They shouted to the gates, as though to make them wider in order to let the Lord in! Re-enact the enthusiasm of this scene. Divide the congregation down the middle and have them turn to face each other. Listen to someone reading the first six verses and then lead the two sides in shouting verses 7-10:

A: Lift up your heads, O you gates; be lifted up, you ancient doors, that the King of glory may come in.
B: Who is this King of glory?
A: The Lord strong and mighty, the Lord mighty in battle.
B: Lift up your heads, O you gates; be lifted up, you ancient doors, that the King of glory may come in.
A: Who is he, this King of glory?
B: The Lord strong and mighty, the Lord mighty in battle.

Patterns of worship
Take the opportunity to follow in your own worship the six-part pattern of worship referred to earlier:
1 Music - Sing some of the praise songs listed above, finishing with a quiet, reflective one.
2 Quiet - Hold a short period of silence (apart from the smallest children!) during which everyone can reflect on how great God is.
3 Prayer - One person should lead a prayer, asking that the Lord will bless your church, allowing it to grow as new people in the district begin to want to worship him.
4 Offerings - Either take a financial offering at this point, or refer to the direct giving scheme that the church operates and commit it to God.
5 Eating - Pass around some sweets, grapes, cherries or whatever is appropriate.
6 Dancing - Either sing a lively song that allows the congregation a chance to move, or invite a dance group to present a piece in worship of God.

Creative praise
On a wall, display a large piece of paper bearing the words of Psalm 132:9b: 'Lord, may your people shout for joy!' (GNB) Give everyone in the congregation a sheet of A5 paper, and ask them to draw themselves on it, praising God. When this is done, ask all the children to collect up the drawings and help you arrange them

on the wall, using glue sticks (put glue on the large picture, not the individual ones), as if they were part of the procession behind the Covenant Box. While they do this, adults can sing hymns which will give them joy in praising God, but which would be beyond the comprehension of the children. When the wall picture is complete, dedicate it to God by reading Psalm 132:1-9, the congregation joining in the last sentence.

Praise chant
God has filled the earth with beauty.
All the world give God your praises.
Worship is your joy and duty.
All the world give God your praises.
Who filled up the sea with water?
All the world give God your praises.
Made each child a son or daughter?
All the world give God your praises.
Made cows moo and set snakes hissing?
All the world give God your praises.
Who invented hugs and kisses?
All the world give God your praises.
Who decided stars would twinkle?
All the world give God your praises.
Eyes would wink and foreheads wrinkle?
All the world give God your praises.
Whose idea were films and telly?
All the world give God your praises.
Who makes stilton cheese so smelly?
All the world give God your praises.
Only God could be that clever,
All the world give God your praises.
Let his praises sound forever.
All the world give God your praises.

worship worshipping God

OUTLINE 31

SERVICE THEME
What happens when we pray?

CHRISTIAN THEME
Worship

BIBLE BASE
Acts 4:23–31; 12:1–19

ALL-AGE SERVICE SUMMARY
Reflecting on a prayer offered by the early church, the congregation will hear that when we talk to God, we can say 'thanks', 'sorry' and 'please'.

THIS WEEK'S RESOURCES
As the theme of the service is prayer, try to introduce several different ways of praying, especially those which will not be so familiar to your congregation.

Setting the scene

Prepare a cassette recording that sounds like a telephone answering machine (or use a real one!). Record several messages using different voices, eg 'Hi, *(your name)*, this is Bob. I just called to say thanks for all you've done this week - give me a ring sometime', or '*(your name)*, you must be out. It's Jenny. I just phoned to say sorry about last night', or 'Where have you been *(your name)*? You haven't been in touch for ages! I've got some things I need to ask you. Ring me. It's your mother'.

Enthuse about how good the telephone is for keeping in touch. Ask what people might think you should do about the messages, in the hope that you will get the reply, 'Answer them!' A phone needs someone on both ends. Does anyone get frustrated when they find themselves speaking to an answerphone? And of course, having a phone and not using it is a waste. Today's service will help us think about keeping in touch, not with your friends but with God, who never goes out and leaves us with just an answerphone message. Read Psalm 77:1.

Bible reading
Acts 4:23–31

Begin with an introduction that summarises the conflict which began with the healing of the lame man and briefly touches on Acts 3:14,21. The reader should try to capture the spirit of boldness in which the believers prayed.

Bible teaching for all ages

Before the service, draw seventeen outlines of teaspoons (or use plastic teaspoons with stickers attached. In the bowl of each write a letter so that the words 'THANKS', 'SORRY' and 'PLEASE' can be made up from them. Then hide them around the room.

Refer back to the Bible reading. What did Peter and John do when they were at last free after surviving their tough time? They went straight back to the other believers and told them what had happened. And what did the believers do? They kept in touch with God. The early church knew how important it was. It is every bit as important for us today.

Tell the congregation that you were going to use some teaspoons to help them remember the importance of prayer, but you have lost them. Ask for help from the children to find them. When all the letters have been brought to the front of the room, find the T and ask whether anyone can make a word beginning with T using the other letters. Do the same at each stage to make 'sorry' and 'please'.

Thanks
God has given us many things to be thankful for. Ask for suggestions. Point out that in the Bible verses, the believers were thankful that God was the ruler and creator of the universe (v 24). He loves us to remember to give him thanks.

Sorry
We all do wrong things which spoil our friendship with God, even though they may not seem as terrible as those done by the men and women who opposed and hated Jesus (v 27). We need to ask God to forgive us.

Please
We say this word when we ask for things. God is the most perfect parent and wants us to ask him for the things we need. What did the Christians (vs 29,30) ask God for? We can ask him for that too, or anything else that is on our minds. Keep just the T, S and P on display. These letters are short for the word 'teaspoon' which is a short way of remembering the three things we can say to God.
If your budget allows it, give each member of the congregation a plastic spoon to take home as their reminder to keep in touch with God.

Ideas for music

Choose songs and hymns which are themselves prayers of thanks, confession or intercession, or those which encourage people to pray. Examples:

'Ask, ask, ask'
'Father God in heaven'
'Our Father who is (art) in heaven'
'I lift my eyes up to the mountains'
'Oh lead me'
'Restore O Lord, the honour of your name'
'Peter and John went to pray'
'What a friend we have in Jesus'

Prayers

Psalm 66

Adapted from Psalm 66:1-4,16-20.

Praise God with shouts of joy all people! Sing to the glory of his name! God has indeed heard me.
He has listened to our prayer.
Say to God, 'How wonderful are the things you do! Your power is so great that your enemies bow down before you.' God has indeed heard me.
He has listened to our prayer.
Everyone on earth worships you, Lord; they sing praises to your name. God has indeed heard me.
He has listened to our prayer.
Come and listen, all who honour God, and I will tell you what he has done for me. God has indeed heard me.
He has listened to our prayer.
I cried to him for help; I praised him with songs. God has indeed heard me.
He has listened to our prayer.
If I had ignored my sins, the Lord would not have heard me, but God has indeed heard me.
He has listened to our prayer.
I praise God, because he does not reject my prayer, nor keep back his constant love for me. God has indeed heard me.
He has listened to our prayer.

Intercessions

Structure a prayer time in the way described above - thanks (and praise), sorry (confession) and please (intercession). If appropriate hold up cut-outs of teaspoons with the letters T, S and P on them to act as visual aids.

Action Prayer

Rehearse the three actions of this prayer, and invite the congregation to adopt the appropriate pose at each stage. At (1) hands raised; at (2) head bowed; at (3) palms upward.

Father God, we thank you (1) for your love for us, which will never let us down. We are sorry (2) for the times when we have forgotten to talk with you, so forgive us, we pray. Please (3) help us as we *(mention any specific church or wider needs)*. Amen.

Prayer board

Start or develop a prayer board on which children and adults may post their prayer requests. Provide paper (or card) and pins, and encourage people to look regularly at the board and pray. (If the board is being used over a long period, appoint someone to make sure that outdated requests are removed or replaced.)

worshipping God

orship *worship*

worship

OUTLINE 32

SERVICE THEME
Psalms help us express our feelings

CHRISTIAN THEME
Worship

BIBLE BASE
Psalm 84; 137

ALL-AGE SERVICE SUMMARY
Two contrasting psalms help both children and adults discover the nature and value of poetry and song in the Bible.

THIS WEEK'S RESOURCES
For many people, especially for children, the most familiar parts of the Bible are the narrative passages. This week, select items which will whet the congregation's appetite for a wider use of psalms (and other poetry) in both public and private worship.

Setting the scene

To introduce today's theme of the Bible's songbook, play a game called 'Name that Tune!' Ask a keyboard player to play the first two notes of a well-known hymn or song - then three notes, then four, and so on until someone in the congregation recognises correctly what it is. Make sure that the three or four songs chosen for this activity reflect the range of ages in the congregation. Invite the congregation to tell their immediate neighbours the name of a Christian song that is particularly significant to them, and explain why it is a favourite. Ask the adults of the congregation to help the youngest members of the congregation to feel included in this as well.

After a couple of minutes, explain that songs have always played an important part in the worship of God. The first mention of music-making in the Bible is in Genesis 4, where a man named Jubal became a harp and flute player (v 21). The last mention is the singing in heaven, where the praise to God will be so perfect that it sounds like a roaring waterfall and loud peals of thunder (Revelation 19:6). In between, there are hundreds of references to people singing in praise of God, including Jesus (Matthew 26:30). And in the same way that this church uses a songbook, whether it is on paper or on overhead projector acetates, the people of Israel had a songbook. It can be found in the Bible, as we will all find out later!

Bible reading
Psalm 84

To emphasise the psalm's musical quality, play a recording of the setting of the first verses of the psalm from Brahms' *A German Requiem* or another setting of the psalm. Play about thirty seconds of the piece, then reduce the volume of the music slightly while the words of the psalm are read. When the reading is finished, raise the volume again for a few seconds, before fading it to silence.

Bible teaching for all ages

Ask six volunteers to help you. Explain that you are going to whisper an adjective which they have to mime for the rest of the congregation, who will guess what it is. The six words you use should be happy, confused, angry, sorry, desperate, sad. Sometimes it is easy to show our feelings, but sometimes we find it hard. To help us explain our feelings to him, God has put an amazing book of songs in the Bible. They are the psalms, and they come from the hymn book which was used in the Temple in Jerusalem.

Prepare six cardboard masks to show happiness, sadness, desperation, sorrow, anger and confusion. These should be circles cut from card about the size of a dinner plate, and held on a stick (see page 76). We have all sorts of feelings - and sometimes they can change really quickly.

Give the happy mask to the first volunteer and ask her to hold it in front of her face. Ask the congregation to consider: 'Is it right to talk about this feeling to God in prayers and in our singing?' Take a vote. Of course it is. Read out examples of happiness from the psalms, as suggested below. Then repeat the process for each of the six feelings - perhaps there will be a more divided opinion over whether confusion and anger are appropriate when we are in conversation with God.

Happy Psalm 84:12
Sad Psalm 137:1
Desperate Psalm 88:1,2
Sorry Psalm 51:1,2
Confused Psalm 137:4
Angry Psalm 137:8

The hymn book of the Jews shows us that God is prepared for us to come to him with all kinds of feelings. Sometimes we wear masks to disguise what we feel, but the writers of the psalms had no masks at all (the volunteers can drop their masks at this point). God was happy that they were honest with him. It can be the same for us - to take out our anger on God is better than to express it to a person who does not deserve it. To tell God that we are in a desperate state is sometimes the only thing we can do, and when we are full of joy, he wants to share that too. And if we can't think of our own words, then the psalms are there to tell us what to say to God. He loved the songs of his people of old; he loves them still today.

Ideas for music

Choose songs and hymns about having a relationship with God, which express love for him or remind the congregation of God's love for them. Verse settings of psalms would also be suitable. Examples:
'God is our Father'
'I love you, Lord, and I lift my voice'
'God of grace'
'Over the mountains and the sea'
'I will sing about your love'
'Sing praise to the Lord/O praise ye the Lord'

New songs

Try encouraging young (or older!) people in the church to write songs of their own. Accompaniments can be added later by church musicians if necessary. The psalms are a good source of material for lyrics, eg Psalms 47, 95, 100, 150. The best ones could be sung in an all-age service at a later date.

Interview

If you have a song-writer or poet (not necessarily someone who does it for a living) in your congregation, ask him or her to talk for a few moments about how they get their inspiration. Is it the Creator God who makes them creative? If you are planning well in advance, perhaps he or she could compose something especially for your congregation.

Prayers

Acclamation
Based on Ephesians 5:19,20

We will praise the Lord.
We will sing hymns and psalms with praise in our hearts.
We will give thanks to our God for everything he has done.
We will praise the Lord together.

Intercessions
Use the song by Graham Kendrick, 'O Lord, the clouds are gathering', as the basis for this prayer. The verse should be sung by a soloist or small group, then as an instrumental verse is played, items for prayer, related to the verse should be read. The congregation then joins in singing the chorus as a response to the petitions.

Action psalm

Read Psalm 99:1-5, encouraging the congregation to accompany it with hand actions (in this way even the youngest children may share in the corporate praise). They should be demonstrated by a group first, then copied by everyone, remaining seated as the psalm is read.

Verse 1a: Both hands pointed upward, high above head.
Verse 1b: Hands trembling.
Verse 2: Sweep hands in wide arc to the sides.
Verse 3: Cup hands together and raise them.
Verse 4: Clench fists.
Verse 5: Put hands together in prayerful attitude and kneel or bow heads; hold this position in silence for a few seconds.

© Mary Hawes

faith in God

OUTLINE 33

SERVICE THEME
Jesus' work on earth reveals who he is

CHRISTIAN THEME
Faith in God

BIBLE BASE
John 9

ALL-AGE SERVICE SUMMARY
Taking as a starting point the account of the healing of a blind man from John's Gospel, the service explores the idea of 'seeing' Jesus, the light of the world, as Christ and Lord.

THIS WEEK'S RESOURCES
As the theme is complex, remember to include items which are visual and interactive, especially if there will be a large proportion of younger children.

Setting the scene

On the deck of an overhead projector, place about twelve small objects with a distinctive outline (a key, a button, a pencil, a cassette, a paper clip, and so on). Include among them a pair of spectacles. Switch the projector on and ask the congregation to use their eyes carefully and look at what is there. After a few seconds, switch it off, rearrange the objects, remove the spectacles, and switch it on again. Ask everyone to decide, in conversation with the person next to them, what you have removed.

After inviting guesses, reveal the spectacles. How wonderfully God has made our eyes! And what a wonderful way he gave humans the skill to restore clarity of sight when it wears out. The Bible is a bit like a pair of glasses. We all have a vague idea of who Jesus was, but when we read the Bible the fullness of who he was and is comes into focus. That is one of the reasons that its authors wrote the New Testament. Having a Bible and not using it is a bit like owning a pair of glasses but preferring to bump into the furniture. Read Psalm 119:18, first explaining it and then as a prayer for everyone as they hear today's teaching.

Bible reading
John 9:1-11

The reader should pause after reading verse 5, while someone else steps forward and lights a single candle, which will serve as a reminder of Christ, 'the light of the world' during the rest of the service.

Bible teaching for all ages

On an acetate, trace or photocopy the image on page 79. Show it on an overhead projector and ask the congregation to talk to those sitting near them to work out what the picture is. Ask for suggestions. Depending on how you look at it, the picture either shows a charming young lady in a hat looking away to the left, or a lady with a big nose looking downwards. Depending on how we look, we see different things.

Remind the congregation of the story of Jesus healing the blind man. You would think that when they saw this miracle, everyone would be convinced that Jesus was the Messiah. But they were divided.

The Pharisees refused to believe it, even though their own eyes showed them that he had performed a miracle. The blind man came to call him Lord after a considerable time thinking and talking about it (v38). His parents were too scared of what people might think to comment on what they really thought.

Sometimes, you hear people say,

'If only I could met Jesus in person, I would have no doubts that it is right to worship him.' But, as you can see, it was not as easy as that even for the people who met him face to face.

When you look at Jesus in the New Testament, you can look at him in two ways, just like an optical illusion. Either you will see a good man who was a great teacher and a fine example - but just a man who died and was gone. Or you see Jesus the Lord, God himself in human form, who came to save our world and give us eternal life.

Christians believe that Jesus was more than a good man - that he died and rose from the dead in order to forgive our sins and restore our friendship with God.

Only if Jesus was God could he have done and said such things. Perhaps people who do not see that have their own kind of blindness, which God is longing to change. People who recognise who Jesus really is have no alternative but to acknowledge him as Christ and worship him as Lord.

Drama

Two people - one in bright light and one in a shadowy corner. The one in shadow is completely blinded by a cloth wrapped around his or her eyes.
A: Come over here.
B: Over where?
A: Into the light.
B: What light?

A: It's light over here.

B: There's no light over there.

A: There is. You just can't see it.

B: I can see all I need to see.

A: I can help you see more.

B: I'm quite happy as I am, thank you.

A: You'll fall over.

B: I won't.

A: You miss out on so many marvellous things.

B: I don't.

A: I've got something for you.

B: Will I like it?

A: You won't know until you come and see, will you?

B: I'll just have a glimpse. I'm not committing myself. (Walks the wrong way.)

A: You're going in the wrong direction.

B: I knew that. (Turns around and walks to A.)

A: There. Isn't that much brighter and better?

B: It looks all the same to me.

A: Well, take your blindfold off.

B: I don't want to.

A: You'll see more.

B: I can see all I want to see.

A: You're lying.

B: How dare you!

A: The truth is, you can't take it off.

B: Don't make me laugh!

A: I can take it off for you.

B: How do you mean?

A: There are some things I can do that you can't do for yourself.

B: I don't see...

A: Aha!

B: I mean I don't see how you can possibly do anything for me that I can't do for myself.

A: You will never know until you trust me.

B: What makes you think I'd do that?

A: The fact that you are in darkness and I am light.

B: What do you think you are? God's gift!

A: Aha!

B: I'm leaving.

A: That's OK. You're free to go.

B: See you!

A: Not unless I help you.

B: Very funny. I meant goodbye. (Walks straight into A's arms.)

A: Hello.

B: There's no escaping you.

A: That's true, although you can fool yourself that you can.

B: That's why the darkness suits me better.

A: Why exactly do you like the darkness so much more than the light?

B: Well now, let me see...

A: Was that a request?

B: For goodness' sake, will you leave me alone?

A: For goodness' sake, I won't leave you alone.

B: If I let you take the blindfold off will you leave me alone?

A: Now that's a really silly question.

B: Why?

A: Because if I take the blindfold off you won't want to leave me alone.

B: What makes you so sure?

A: I've seen it all before.

B: Go on then. Let me see what you can do! (A carefully takes the cloth from B's eyes. As it opens out, the word 'sins' is revealed on it. A takes it away and puts it in a pocket. B's eyes open slowly and a broad smile appears on his/her face. Turning to look at A, his/her expression changes quickly to awe. He/she kneels at A's feet.)

Ideas for music

Choose songs and hymns about Jesus, his life and work and our relationship with him today. Examples:

'Come to Jesus, he's amazing'
'From heaven you came'
'Where there once was only hurt'
'Lord, you are the light of the world'
'Lord you were rich/thou wast rich'
'Make way, make way'

Prayers

Musical prayer

Sing 'Open our eyes, Lord'. The words should be sung twice, with an instrumental verse between the two. While the instruments are playing, someone should read the prayer of Richard of Chichester:

O, most merciful redeemer, friend and brother, may we see you more clearly, love you more dearly, follow you more nearly, day by day.

Psalm 146

In this arrangement of verses 1,2 and 7 to 10, the congregation responds to the leader with the repeated line:

Praise the Lord! Praise the Lord, O my soul!
I will praise him as long as I live.

He upholds the cause of the oppressed.
I will praise him as long as I live.
He gives food to the hungry.
I will praise him as long as I live.
The Lord gives sight to the blind.
I will praise him as long as I live.
He lifts up those who are bowed down.
I will praise him as long as I live.
The Lord loves his righteous people.
I will praise him as long as I live.
He cares for the strangers, the widows and the orphans.
I will praise him as long as I live.
The Lord is king for ever. Praise the Lord!
I will praise him as long as I live.

Sights of praise

Show a series of slides from someone's holiday photograph collection. Ask people to pray with their eyes open as someone speaks words of praise from the psalms or spontaneous praise is offered. Conclude with a prayer thanking God for eyesight itself.

Intercessions

Pray for those who are blind and the charities which seek to help them. Pray for those who are blind as to who Jesus is, including a silence for the congregation to name before God particular people, and pray for opportunities for their 'eyes to be open'.

Seeing Jesus

Jesus, I look to you, light driving out the darkness,
Jesus I look to you, beauty among the ugliness,
Jesus I look to you, colour illuminating the greyness,
Jesus I look to you, focus making clear my doubts,
Jesus I look to you, bright hope ending my dismay,
Jesus I look to you, sunrise at the end of my night,
Shine on me, Jesus, light of the world.

faith in God

OUTLINE 34

SERVICE THEME
Can we remove wrongdoing and guilt?

CHRISTIAN THEME
Faith in God

BIBLE BASE
Luke 5:17–26; Romans 3:22–26; 5:1–11

ALL-AGE SERVICE SUMMARY
We look at the Christian answer to the problem of wrongdoing and guilt, contrasting them with answers given by other faiths and learn that only believing in Jesus will work.

THIS WEEK'S RESOURCES
Although this is a serious subject, activities which are fun need not be rejected. They will help to reinforce the message and will help everyone to remember the theme after the service.

Setting the scene

Without telling them that you are asking the impossible, invite three children or young people to the front of the room and give them challenges.

The first is to crouch down in front of a step of some kind, hold tightly to his shoes and pull himself up on the step by yanking his feet in the air.

The second must simply read a word: 'Forgive'. The snag is that the word is written on paper stuck to her nose (or pinned to the middle of her back) so that she is unable to read it.

The third is given a paper shaped as shown on page 81. He should hold the paper at A and B, and pull it into three parts at one attempt.

After they have struggled unsuccessfully, show them that there are three easy solutions. Lift the child on to the step, read the word for the girl, and hold the paper in the centre allowing the outside parts to be torn away. Easy! There is no possible way they could have fulfilled those challenges by their own efforts - the only solution was to allow someone else to do it for them.

In the same way, today we will all learn about something only Jesus can do for us - no one can possibly do it for themselves. Read Acts 10:43 as a trailer.

Bible reading
Romans 3:22–26

This reading is rather abstract for an all-age audience, so ask a group of people to practise and then perform simple actions which will help the message to get across visually. For example, during verse 22, they could stretch out their arms to form a cross shape, moving their arms down as though to embrace someone.

Bible teaching for all ages

The visual aid you need for this talk is most easily prepared on an overhead projector, but a white board or a piece of formica can be used. On an acetate, draw the outline of a unisex figure (or gingerbread man shape). Place this face down on the deck of the projector.

Talk about sin putting humans out of touch with God and read Romans 3:23. Write the word 'Sins' on the acetate with *permanent* (spirit-based) projector pen across the chest of the figure, but, of course, on the other side of the plastic to the figure.

Produce three bottles of coloured fluid, each of which represents one of the ways in which humans have tried to deal with the problem of sin. The first is labelled 'Trying to be good' (it contains water coloured red with food dye). Speak of people's hope that, if they are good enough, God will let them into heaven. Mention that Muslims hope that by praying five times a day, giving to the poor, fasting and going on a pilgrimage, they will be good enough. Put some of the red liquid on a tissue and try to erase 'Sins' with it. Nothing will happen.

The second bottle is labelled 'Attempting to please God' and contains water dyed blue. Speak of how Sikhs have a long set of rules laid down by their leaders six centuries ago, and the signs they wear (including uncut hair which is why they cover it with a turban) to remind them. Others hope that by going to church occasionally, they will make God happy. The second fluid fails to clean away 'Sins'.

The third bottle is labelled 'Asking for God's forgiveness'. The purple liquid this contains is methylated spirit. Talk of how Jesus' life, death and resurrection have made God's forgiveness available to all who ask for it. Read Romans 3:25-26 and try out the fluid. It will wipe away 'Sins', but leave the human figure in place. Challenge the congregation to turn to God and say sorry, the only way to restore friendship with God.

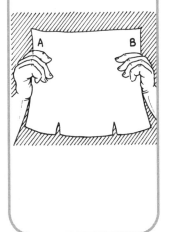

Memory verse

As a church, learn this verse: '...all who have faith in Jesus will have their sins forgiven in his name' Acts 10:43 (CEV). Display it on an overhead projector or board and repeat it, erasing one word each time.

Ideas for music

Choose songs and hymns about God's love, mercy and forgiveness. Examples:

'God forgave my sin in Jesus' name'
'God is good'
'Praise my soul the king of heaven'
'See Christ wounded for our sake'
'Such love'
'The price is paid'
'There is a green hill far away'
'There is no condemnation'
'Wide, wide as the ocean'

Prayers

Confession

Lord God, as we look back over our lives, there have been things we should not have done. We are truly sorry.
Please forgive us.

Things we should have done and didn't. We are truly sorry.
Please forgive us.

Things we should not have said. We are truly sorry.
Please forgive us.

Things we should have said, but couldn't be bothered. We are truly sorry.
Please forgive us.

Things we should not have thought. We are truly sorry.
Please forgive us.

Things we should have thought of, but forgot. We are truly sorry.
Please forgive us.

Say a song

To help people focus on the words of a well-known song, say it instead of (or before) singing it as a prayer. Either the congregation says it together or the leader says the verses and everyone else joins in with the chorus or some other arrangement suited to the song chosen. 'Such love', 'There is a green hill' or 'The price is paid' would be suitable.

faith in God

h in God

OUTLINE 35

SERVICE THEME
Following God, putting faith in him alone

CHRISTIAN THEME
Faith in God

BIBLE BASE
Genesis 12:1–9; 15:1–6

ALL-AGE SERVICE SUMMARY
Using the story of Abraham, the service encourages the congregation, both as individuals and together, to put their trust in God because he loves us and wants the best for us.

THIS WEEK'S RESOURCES
Make the most of the active and visual parts of the service to keep the younger members of the congregation involved.

Setting the scene

Show a telephone which has a 'secrecy' button and explain that the theme of the service is trust. The telephone you use requires trust. It has a button on it which allows you to talk to someone else in the room 'in secrecy' without the person on the end of the line hearing. Give a humorous example of how you might use it:

'Hello, Great-Aunt Matilda, and how are you? *(Exaggerate pressing the secrecy button.)* She's the one who gave me those ghastly pink and purple spotty socks for my birthday. *(Take your finger off the button.)* How kind of you to remember my birthday! Did I like the socks? Aunty, dear, *like* isn't a strong enough word to express my feelings.'

Explain that every time you press the secrecy button you have to trust that the machine really works. The man in today's story put his trust in God so completely that he decided to do just what God had told him, even though he couldn't see him. Every time we pray, we are trusting that God is listening to us. We cannot be sure, because we cannot see him, but we trust that he hears us. Read Psalm 62:8. When you want someone to talk to, you can turn to God with as much trust as you turn to the telephone!

Bible reading
Genesis 11:31 – 12:9

During the reading, display a map of the Middle East (see page 83) on an overhead projector. Cut out a silhouette figure of Abraham. At the beginning of the reading, place it on Ur. At appropriate points, move it to Haran, Shechem, Bethel and Canaan.

Bible teaching for all ages

The two other visual aids (page 83) will help you give this talk. They are designed to transfer directly onto acetate by using an ordinary photocopier with special coarser acetates.

Tell the story contained in Genesis 15:1–6, introducing Abraham (use his familiar name to avoid confusion) as a wealthy and elderly man whose great sadness was that he had no children. God called him to do exactly as he said, assuring him that he had a good plan for him. Abraham trusted God, even though he could not see him, and obeyed. He began a long journey to the new home God wanted to give him. God gave him a remarkable promise - he would have more children, grandchildren and descendants than there are stars in the sky. Abraham must have known that this was very, very unlikely, but he trusted God. This trust pleased God, and he accepted him as his friend. Did God fulfil his promise? Yes, he did, but that is another story!

That very same God, who is the only God, calls you to trust him too; to trust him enough to pray to him even though you cannot see him, enough to do what he wants even when it is difficult, enough to be his friend through good times and bad. How can you be sure he is worth trusting? Because he loves you and has the best possible plan for you. The words he said to Abraham (Genesis 15:1) apply to you and me as well.

Ideas for music

Choose songs and hymns about our trust in God and joy in following him.
Examples:
'Guide me, O my great Redeemer'
'I have decided to follow Jesus'
'Beautiful Lord, wonderful Saviour'
'Almighty God, my redeemer'
'Faithful One'
'I'm your child'
'I'm going to take a step of faith'
'One more step along the road'
'The journey of life'

Prayers

Journeying praise

The congregation sit and join in the italic lines of these verses of praise, in response to the leader. Establish a marching rhythm by encouraging everyone to slap their hands on their knees - left, right, left, right...

Going on a journey,
Forward, forward,
Don't know where,
Forward, forward,
God is going to guide us,
Forward, forward,
Our God cares.
Forward, forward,

God will be our leader,
Following, following,
Everywhere,
Following, following,
Keeping us from danger,
Following, following,
Our God cares,
Following, following,

God has made a promise,
Trusting, trusting,
We're not scared,
Trusting, trusting,
Praise him for he loves us,
Trusting, trusting,
Our God cares,
Trusting, trusting,

Psalm 131

The congregation responds to the leader with the repeated italic line:

Lord, I have given up my pride,
I simply put my trust in you.
I have turned away from
selfish ways,
I simply put my trust in you.
I am not concerned with
complicated matters,
I simply put my trust in you.
Instead I am content and at peace,
I simply put my trust in you,
Like a child lying in its
mother's arms,
I simply put my trust in you.
So I am quiet in your presence,
I simply put my trust in you.
(Name of your church) trusts in the
Lord, now and for ever.
I simply put my trust in you. Amen.

Intercessions

Focus on journeys in your prayers. Pray for any in the congregation who are travelling in the near future, including any who travel as part of their missionary service. Pray for safety for commuters, children on their way to school, and distance drivers.

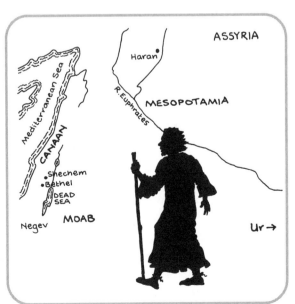

faith

christian life

christian

OUTLINE 36

SERVICE THEME
God offers his people a new start

CHRISTIAN THEME
The Christian life

BIBLE BASE
Ezekiel 36:22 - 37:14

ALL-AGE SERVICE SUMMARY
The service uses two metaphors for the renewing work of the Holy Spirit. Firstly, the connection is made between the potential in a dead-looking seed and the potential in each person. Secondly, the story of the valley of dead bones is used to bring home God's continuing promise of new life and hope for his people.

THIS WEEK'S RESOURCES
This part of Bible history may not be familiar to some of the congregation, especially its younger members. Take care to explain the situation faced by the Jews in exile in Babylon without giving too much time to it at the expense of the activities which make God's message relevant to today.

Setting the scene
Show an apple and announce a competition to guess how many seeds there are inside it. Slice it up, count the seeds and declare a winner. Then pose a more difficult question. Hold up one of the seeds and ask, 'How many apples are there inside this seed?' The answer is, of course, uncountable thousands. Wonder at the way God has created the world, teeming with the possibility of life.

But a dry, apparently lifeless seed needs help in order to produce a living apple tree and fruitful apples. Ask the congregation to call out some of the things it needs - earth, rain, materials, warmth, sun, and so on. Read John 12:24.

For all Christians, there come times when we feel exhausted, fed up, dried out. There are two ways of thinking about it. We can either see it as the end - and feel as useless as a thrown-away apple core. Or we can see it as a beginning - because within it are the seeds which, even though they look lifeless, will produce good things to come.

Perhaps you remember that long ago, long before the birth of Jesus the Jews had reached a bitter end in captivity, far away from home in Babylon. But God is in the business of giving new life where there appears to be none. As we shall find out today, Babylon turned out to be, for the Jews, a place where they could grow and be happy, and where the Holy Spirit would allow them to make a new start. If you feel today that you have reached a dried-up state, listen, because God has something to say to you.
Give an apple as a prize to the person who guessed the right number of seeds.

Bible reading
Ezekiel 37:1-14
Before the reading, explain a little about the prophet Ezekiel, especially about the very vivid pictures that God gave him so that he could help others know what God wanted to say and what God wanted to do in their lives. The reading could be split between three readers: one speaking the words of God, one the words of Ezekiel and a third reading everything else.

Bible teaching for all ages
Remind the congregation of the Jews' sad situation. They had been in exile, many miles from their homeland, after a terrible defeat in battle. Introduce three imaginary characters, the Bones family, from that time, showing their pictures reproduced from page 85.

Broken Bones
The disaster, terrible as it was, made this woman realise something. She knew that the way she had behaved, treating God as if he was not there, was a wrong way to live. She came to be bitterly sorry that she had prayed to wooden idols instead of the true God. She told God that things could not get any worse, and asked him to forgive her. And God had a message for her, one which filled her with hope and expectation. Read Ezekiel 36:25,26.

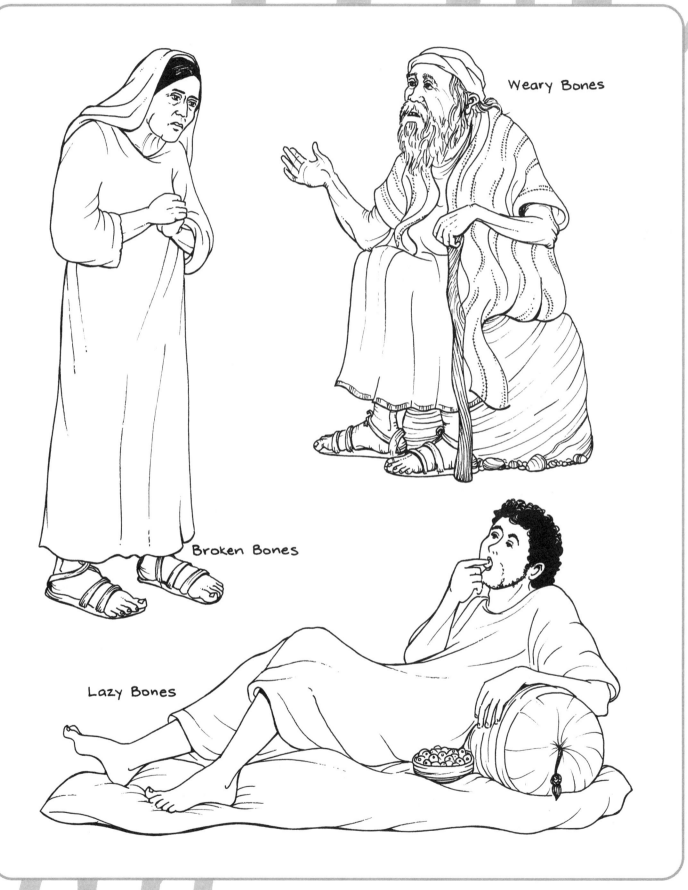

christian life

Lazy Bones

For him, the bad times had come as a severe shock. He had selfishly looked after himself, but done nothing for the good of those around him. God had a message for him as well. Even he would be restored to his homeland. He had done nothing to deserve it - God was doing it because he could not help loving Lazy Bones. Read what it was from Ezekiel 36:32-35a.

Weary Bones

This old man nearly gave up hope. It seemed to him that he would never have strength to survive the hardship of what he was going through. He kept thinking back to the old days when everything seemed so much better. With the world changing so fast he wondered what would become of him. How could those who were left (so few!) ever fulfil the task of rebuilding Jerusalem (so great!). But instead of despairing, he did the most valuable thing he could - he cried to the Lord God for help. Read God's message to him from Ezekiel 36:37,38.

Conclusion

Recount Ezekiel's vision of dry bones coming to life, read earlier from the Bible. Who is it that can give us hope of new life in the way these three people found it? The Holy Spirit of God can. That is the job of the Spirit - to give new life to people who have lost hope, or are worn out, or realise there is a task ahead which is too hard for them to undertake alone. The very same Spirit who gave life and hope to the Jews so long ago will give life and hope to us as well.

Ideas for music

Choose songs and hymns about the new life and hope which the Spirit of God gives us.
Examples:
'Jesus put this song into our hearts'
'O breath of life'
'I am a new creation'
'Is anyone thirsty?'
'It's our confession, Lord'
'Restore, O Lord'
'There's new life in Jesus'
'We need to grow'

Prayers

Seeds of hope

Give everyone a seed (perhaps an apple seed) as a symbol of the potential for life that is available for us all. Invite everyone to think quietly about the week ahead. What are the things they would like to achieve? After a short silence, the leader should pray the words below. Invite everyone to take their seed away from the service and plant it later on that day as a sign to themselves and to God of wanting to please him in the way their life develops from this point onward:

'Creator God, within this seed you have placed the potential for a thousand, thousand apples. Within our lives you have placed the potential for a thousand, thousand possibilities. To live and grow in the way that is best for us we need your help. We ask that your Holy Spirit will breathe through us - through our choices, through our decisions, through our lives. Bring to life in us all that would please you, all that would enrich the world, and all that would be good for us. Amen'.

Bones alive

Invite everyone to sit completely still and relaxed, with their eyes shut. In the silence, ask them to move just one bone of the thumb, and to think how beautifully God has made it. Isaac Newton said, 'In the absence of any other proof, the thumb alone would convince me of the existence of God'.

Go on to ask them to move the whole of their thumb around and around, thanking God all the while for the wonder of the design. One stage at a time, invite everyone to move the rest of their fingers, their wrist, their other hand as well, then all of their arms, with words spoken by the leader which thank God for the way bone is attached to bone with such intricacy. Bring this to a close by asking people to bring their palms together, slowly at first, and then faster until the congregation is delivering a huge round of applause to God for the goodness of the way our bodies are put together.

The breath of the Spirit

Where the Spirit of the Lord is,
There is love for one another.
Where the Spirit of the Lord is,
There is power to make our faith strong.
Where the Spirit of the Lord is,
There is light to help us understand God.
Where the Spirit of the Lord is,
There is freedom in God's family.
Where the Spirit of the Lord is,
There is hope to face the future.
Breathe on us, Holy Spirit, until these dry bones dance to please you.
Breathe on us, Holy Spirit, and bring us all new life.

christian life
christian life

OUTLINE 37

SERVICE THEME
Hearing and responding to the word of God

CHRISTIAN THEME
The Christian life

BIBLE BASE
Luke 8:4–15

ALL-AGE SERVICE SUMMARY
Jesus' story of the sower highlights different reactions to the Word of God and challenges everyone to consider how well the teaching of Jesus is received in our own hearts and lives.

THIS WEEK'S RESOURCES
The story of the sower (or of the soils) lends itself to many different ways of visual presentation. Bear in mind that the youngest children will only be able to engage in the teaching at a literal level and allow them the opportunity simply to thank God for seeds, for growth, etc.

Setting the scene
Show some seeds of different kinds, both large and small. Invite a number of children to guess, as an informal quiz, what grows from each. Encourage them to marvel at what God can make grow from so small a seed. If there are trees nearby, talk about them: 'Each tree near the church started out like one of those tiny seeds.' Praise God for this, perhaps using words based on Psalm 104:13,14. Use this prayer (you may like to link it to an offertory):

'Thank you, our Father God, that you have made such an amazing world. Thank you for each tiny seed and each mighty tree. We offer our small gifts and our little lives into your care, and ask you to do something mighty with them to bring you glory. Amen.'

Bible reading
Luke 8:4–15
If the drama is being used, read Luke 8:8b–15. If it is not being used, split the passage into two readings - verses 4–8, then verses 9–15 with some other activity between them.

Bible teaching for all ages
In advance, you need to prepare a visual aid which consists of a cereal bowl filled with dry *Rice Krispies* and four large buckets, filled in the following ways:

1 Contains soil, covered with flat stones or card on top (to represent the path).
2 Filled with rocks or pebbles.
3 Contains soil, covered with turf (which could be borrowed from a lawn, and returned afterwards).
4 Appears to be full of soil, but concealing a box of *Rice Krispies* attached to a string, which is either hidden just below the surface or brought unobtrusively over the edge of the bucket and concealed with parcel tape.

Invite the congregation to tell you the sound that *Rice Krispies* make. You might be able to get them to chant: 'Snap! Crackle! Pop!' in unison (bearing in mind sensitivities of some people to this kind of thing!). Invite four children, one after another, to try to plant a *Rice Krispie* from the bowl into each bucket. Interview each child as you do so to bring out the following points about the buckets:
1 It is impossible to get the 'seed' into the soil.
2 There is no soil at all.
3 The 'seed' gets lost in the grass.
4 This is good soil where planting is possible. Invite other children to plant *Rice Krispies* in this bucket. Then say that the seeds are already growing, pull the string and enjoy the laughter as a whole box of *Rice Krispies* grows before your eyes.

Tip the contents of the box into a bowl and invite the children to count or guess how many *Rice Krispies* have 'grown'. Read Luke 8:8

to the congregation. Explain that *Rice Krispies* do not really grow, but if you want to hear 'Snap! Crackle! Pop!' you need plenty of them. Jesus was not talking about breakfast cereals, but about the way faith in him grows when people hear his words and think about them 'in their hearts'. Conclude by reading the rap poem which is part of the illustration on page 89.

Growing pains
This drama, by Stephen Deal, is reproduced with permission.
Prepare two bamboo canes by tying several lengths of string to each of them at regular intervals. Attach to the strings paper heads of corn and suitable leaves. Lay the canes across the front of the performing area. When they are lifted horizontally the effect should be of a line of corn growing up. (You may need to weight the bottom of the strings.) The seeds shown in this sketch should be pop corn because it is easily seen and quickly picked up. Narrators A and B stand to the left and right of the 'stage'.

A: A farmer when forth to sew.
B: And when he had finished hemming the curtains, he went to his field to plant some seeds.
A: Like so. *(A farmer starts sowing seeds, throwing them to the left and to the right. A and B (in the UK only!) hum the theme tune to 'The Archers' - elsewhere another theme tune associated with farming.)*

B: We would like to draw attention to our farmer's technique. This particular method of sowing seeds is called broadcasting.
A: Which is where the term comes from regarding radio and television.
B: We thought you'd like to know that.
A: In case you didn't already.
B: Some of the seeds fell upon a path.
A: Where they attracted the attention of a herd of birds.
B: A herd? *(A group of children rush in and grab the seeds, preferably with lots of 'tweets' and bird effects. After they have exited, the farmer sows some more seeds.)*
A: And some of the seeds fell on stony ground.
B: The corn grew quickly. *(The first bamboo cane is lifted quickly.)*
A: But the roots could not grow properly because of the stones, and so the corn died. *(The bamboo cane is dropped. Everyone says, 'Ahh'.)*
B: Other seeds grew up among weeds. *(The first bamboo cane is lifted again and people take up position next to the corn.)*
A: And the weeds throttled and strangled and mangled the corn. *(The people tear the corn apart, singing as they do so 'Here we go, here we go, here we go...' in the manner of football hooligans.)*
B: But some of the seed fell upon good soil.
A: And grew to produce corn with as much as a hundred seeds each.

(The second bamboo cane is lifted and held as high as possible.)

Ideas for music

Choose songs and hymns on the theme of growth and harvest, either in the literal sense or in relation to faith or on the theme of the Word of God.
Examples:
'God has spoken to his people'
'One must water, one must weed'
'We have heard a joyful sound'
'We plough the fields and scatter'
'The word of the Lord is planted in my heart'

Prayers

Confession

This prayer, in which the congregation responds to the leader with the italic line, may not be suitable in a setting where some have a serious hearing loss. The repeated line could be adapted to: 'Let us all hear your word in our hearts'.

Jesus said, 'Love your enemies'. *(Silence.)* Those who have ears to hear,
Let us all hear.
Jesus said 'Pray for those who ill-treat you'. *(Silence.)* Those who have ears to hear,
Let us all hear.
Jesus said, 'Give and lend to those who ask you'. *(Silence.)* Those who have ears to hear,
Let us all hear.
Jesus said, 'Be merciful - forgive and you will be forgiven'. *(Silence.)* Those who have ears to hear,
Let us all hear.
Jesus said, 'Why do you call me Lord, but not do what I say?' *(Silence.)*
Those who have ears to hear,
Let us all hear.
Lord Jesus, our sins against our fellow human beings are sins against you. But we want to live as your friends. You said that when your friends come to you in faith, you say, 'Friend, your sins are forgiven'. So we confess our sins and ask you to forgive us. *(Silence.)* Those who have ears to hear,
Let us all hear.

Song of creation

An arrangement by Eileen Turner of the 'Song of Creation' from *The Alternative Service Book*.

Bless the Lord, created things: angels in heaven:
Sing God's praise and exalt him forever.
Clouds in the sky, sun, moon and stars:
Sing God's praise and exalt him forever.
Bless the Lord, light and darkness, rain, dew and wind:
Sing God's praise and exalt him forever.
Frost, ice and snow, lightning and storms:
Sing God's praise and exalt him forever.
Bless the Lord, hills and flat land:
Sing God's praise and exalt him forever.
Plants and animals, fish, birds and people:
Sing God's praise and exalt him forever.

Intercession

Invite first children and then adults to contribute topics for prayer, listing them on an overhead projector. Suggest that the theme of these prayers should be the word taking root, so it is particularly appropriate to pray for missionaries and societies supported by the church. Include also world needs, local needs, and prayers for those who are ill or in trouble. Depending on the tradition of the congregation, lead in open prayer that mentions items on the list and follow it with a time of silence. The Lord's Prayer may be an appropriate way to sum up these intercessions.

At home

Comment on the way people read the cereal packets at the breakfast table. Distribute copies of the illustration on page 89, one per family. Invite them to take it home, talk together about it, and write in the space the names of four or five people for whom they would like to pray, particularly in relation to hearing the good news about Jesus. Suggest that they paste it on their cereal packets so that they can read and pray about it over breakfast each morning.
© Simon Foulkes

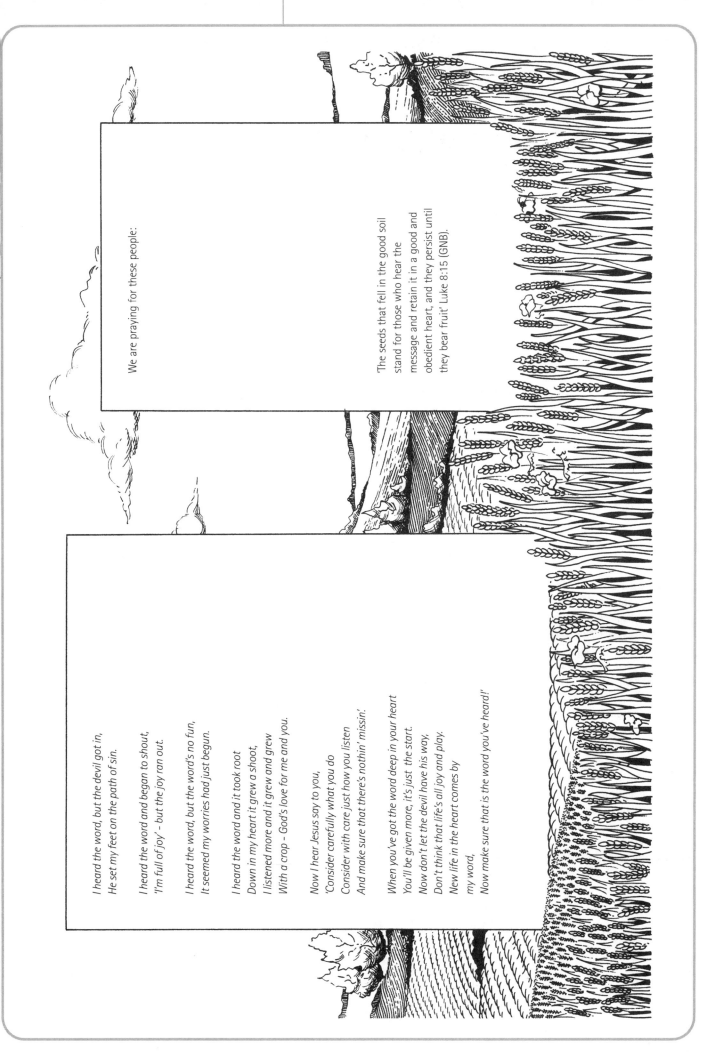

We are praying for these people:

'The seeds that fell in the good soil stand for those who hear the message and retain it in a good and obedient heart, and they persist until they bear fruit' Luke 8:15 (GNB).

I heard the word, but the devil got in,
He set my feet on the path of sin.

I heard the word and began to shout,
'I'm full of joy' – but the joy ran out.

I heard the word, but the word's no fun,
It seemed my worries had just begun.

I heard the word and it took root
Down in my heart it grew a shoot,
I listened more and it grew and grew
With a crop – God's love for me and you.

Now I hear Jesus say to you,
'Consider carefully what you do
Consider with care just how you listen
And make sure that there's nothin' missin'.

When you've got the word deep in your heart
You'll be given more, it's just the start.
Now don't let the devil have his way,
Don't think that life's all joy and play.
New life in the heart comes by
my word,
Now make sure that is the word you've heard!'

christian life

OUTLINE 38

SERVICE THEME
The joy of change

CHRISTIAN THEME
The Christian life

BIBLE BASE
Matthew 5:1-12

ALL-AGE SERVICE SUMMARY
Using the beatitudes, the service focuses on changing to become more what God wants us to be, and helps the congregation to discover to what kind of people Jesus says, 'Congratulations!'

THIS WEEK'S RESOURCES
Keep the service as visual as possible to assist the younger children. They will not, of course, understand everything that is said, but they can learn something about God's acceptance of each individual as they are included in the worship in every way possible.

Setting the scene

This is the story of two teapots. They were brought out of the cupboard to be used at a family celebration. Because it was a splendid occasion, both of them were given a good polish and set on the kitchen table, ready to be used. The first teapot was short, brown and dumpy. She was thrilled with the idea of being part of such a great occasion. The other teapot was tall, thin and shiny. She knew that all the family would be thrilled that she was part of such a great occasion. But that is where the trouble began!

As the boiling water was tipped into the short, brown teapot, she hissed with satisfaction: 'This is what I was born for.' But the tall, shiny teapot absolutely refused to have water poured into her: 'This is a special occasion,' she declared. 'The only thing I am prepared to be filled with is champagne!' Sadly, she got her way!

Well, in the brown teapot the tea was brewed for five minutes and got stronger and stronger. But in the shiny teapot, the champagne stood for five minutes and got flatter and flatter. You can imagine what happened! Everyone was absolutely delighted with the cup of tea they got from the brown teapot. But when they tasted the champagne from the shiny teapot, they nearly spat it out! The brown teapot got filled again and again. The shiny teapot stayed unused on the side.

You see, there are some things in life that we were created to do. Being a follower of Jesus is one of those things! It may not be as enticing as some other ways of living, just as tea is not as sparkling as champagne, but because it is how humans are meant to be, it is the best way! Today we are all going to hear about the way of life Jesus intended for us. And there are some surprises about that as well - things that sometimes get portrayed in life as unfortunate or undesirable are the things to which Jesus says: 'Congratulations!' As we learn from the Bible today, look for things which wouldn't appeal to people who haven't had their lives turned around by Jesus - but actually belong to humans as well as tea belongs in a teapot.

Bible reading
Matthew 5:1-12
Involve two readers, one reading the first part of each beatitude and the other the second.

Bible teaching for all ages

Introduce the theme of 'change' by presenting the first part of the talk as an award-giving ceremony. Explain that certain members of the congregation are going to be given awards to say 'congratulations' for reaching a turning point in life. The awards are certificates. It is probably wisest already to have in mind who will be given the awards (that way you can be sure they will be in church), but you could take impromptu nominations as well.

Make sure the 'turning point' awards are spread over every age represented in the congregation. You could, for instance, give an award for recently being born, for beginning to walk, for starting school, for a new tooth, for getting a job, for getting engaged, for leaving home, for marrying, for having a baby, for being promoted, for a new home, new dress or new responsibility in the church, for retirement, for taking up a new hobby, for a first grandchild, and so on. Open an envelope in the style of the Oscars as you announce each award and give each person a round of applause as they receive their certificate. Be sure to say, 'Congratulations.'

Then turn your attention to Matthew 5:1-12 and ask, 'To whom does Jesus say congratulations?' What a surprise! It is not to the sort of people you would expect at all!

ristian life

Jesus' awards go to those who are sad at the moment, those who are not full of themselves, those who work at making peace between people, those who are given a rough time because they are Christians. Congratulations to them!

Jesus' awards go to people who have reached turning points. But they don't work the way the 'Oscars' do! They are for people who have come to their senses and decided to change and go Jesus' way.
* They want what God wants, not selfish things.
* They want what is fair, even if that costs them.
* They know that when life hurts, God is close.
* They live to help others, because that brings them joy.

All turning-point celebrations have a down-side as well as an up-side. Cutting your first tooth is a wonderful achievement, but it is painful. Leaving home is good, but it is scary. Retirement is a good thing at the end of a working life, but it takes some getting used to. The same is true of Jesus' awards. Sometimes they are for things that go unrewarded in life, even painful things. But to people who have discovered the thrill of the revolutionary way Jesus can change their lives around, they are a true blessing!

Ideas for music
Choose songs and hymns about personal commitment to following Jesus and about the change that this decision makes in our lives. Examples:
'I have decided to follow Jesus'
'I want to walk with Jesus Christ'
'I want to serve the purpose of God'
'Lord, I come to you'
'O Jesus, I have promised'
'Nothing but the love of Jesus'
'Now thank we all our God'
'What made a difference in the life of Saul?'
'Will you come and follow me?'

Prayers
Thanksgiving
During the week before the service, ask ten people to help you prepare prayers of thanks. Give each of them an overhead projector acetate and a couple of OHP pens. Make sure that you offer the chance to a cross-section of ages, adult, teenage and children. Ask them to draw on the acetate something for which they would like to thank God this week (one or two words may be added for clarity, but the prayers should be principally pictorial). Collect them before the service and create a further acetate which reads: 'Thank you, Lord God.' Play suitable music as you show the acetates with the written one at the beginning and the end. ('Thank you for hearing me' by Sinead O'Connor from the album *Universal Mother* could be used, showing one acetate during each section. An alternative song to use might be 'Thank U' by Alanis Morissette from the album *Supposed Former Infatuation Junkie*. Make sure that you listen to the songs first to check that they would be suitable for your congregation.)

Prayer of response
Jesus taught us to stop being selfish and learn to want what God wants, but sometimes that is hard.
Loving Jesus, help us to change.
Jesus taught us to want what is fair, even if it costs us, but sometimes that is hard.
Loving Jesus, help us to change.
Jesus taught us to realise that God is close, even when life hurts, but sometimes that is hard.
Loving Jesus, help us to change.
Jesus taught us to help others, because that brings them joy, but sometimes that is hard.
Loving Jesus, help us to change.
So that we will be changed;
And our church will be changed;
And our town will be changed;
And our land will be changed;
And the whole world will be changed;
For the glory of God. Amen.

christian life

Setting the scene

This story is told with grateful thanks to the magazine of the Church Mission Society. Goruganthula Narayanamurti lived in South India at the end of the nineteenth century. He was a Hindu. As a high caste Brahmin, he came into contact with Christian missionaries. More than anything else, it was the kindness they showed in their way of life which impressed him. This meant that when he was talking with them, the subject of conversation passed naturally to their search for truth. His family were very angry and beat him severely. However, this only served to make him more curious about Jesus, whom the Christians worshipped. What was so powerful about Jesus that made his family try to stop him finding out? He began to read the Bible.

When his family found out about this, they locked him in a coal shed without food or water, to bring him to his senses. After three days, he broke the door down and ran away. He was sure God was with him in this adventure, because he found a bag with a small amount of money in it. It was just enough to buy food to stop him starving and to pay his fare to escape across the river on a ferry.

He made his way to the home of a missionary and he was baptised on 8 June 1890. He wrote, 'It was not [debating about Jesus] with the missionaries that convinced me of the gospel; it was that very [evident] love of God [shown] in and through their hands and hearts'.

Now the story comes right up to date! Becoming a Christian meant that he lost all his family and property, but he got a new job with the Christian church. He had children, who also grew up as Christians, and he also had a grandson who crossed the sea as a missionary to England. His name is Rev Sam Prasadam, and he has been a vicar of a parish in Luton, north of London. He says, 'Our ministry in this multi-faith and multi-cultural [area] is our way of saying thank you to the Church Missionary Society and to the churches as a whole for bringing the Christian gospel to India'.

Bible reading
Acts 10:1–33

This is a complex story and would benefit from presentation by five readers: a narrator, an angel (and the Spirit), Cornelius, Peter, a representative of the three servants. Have two locations for the reading, with the servant crossing from one to the other during verse 8, and back with Peter during verse 23.

Bible teaching for all ages

As you begin to give the talk, draw a large, freehand circle (this can be done either on an overhead projector or a flip chart). As you continue, add eyes, ears and a mouth in order to create a human face. There is no illustration to follow because, in a sense, the rougher the drawing is, the better! The idea is to create a face that could represent any man, woman or child in the congregation. References are to Acts 10.

Eyes to see the vision

In Peter's case, it was literally a vision, and a strange one (v 10). The vision was for someone to enable the good news about Jesus to be spread among people who had never heard before - the Gentiles. Today, the vision might be equally dramatic, or just a growing sense given by the Holy Spirit to someone that there is a job to be done for God that exactly fits him or her.

Ears to listen to need

It is very clear that Peter did not go into this job as if he knew everything and the people he went to knew nothing (vs 25,26). He went as a servant, to find out what the needs of the people really were. That is very important for today's missionaries as well, since a lot of damage has been done by people who took the message of Jesus in an insensitive way to places where it wasn't appreciated. However, the world is full of need - for teachers, health workers, farming advisers, engineers, those who understand finance. Very often, mission work means displaying the practical love of Jesus through the way these things are offered to people who really need them.

A mouth to tell the story

When Cornelius recognised that Peter was a godly man, he genuinely wanted to hear about Jesus, the one whom Peter worshipped (v 33). When Peter described Jesus, the result was that Cornelius and his household became Christians and were transformed by the Holy Spirit (vs 44-48). What a joy for them, and for all the Gentiles (like us) who came after them! That is what mission work is still about today - making people's lives better when they discover the fullness of what Jesus wants to do for them.

Conclusion

So who could be a missionary? Anyone who loves Jesus. Even you! Does this face look like you at all?

Ideas for music

Choose songs and hymns about God's call to tell the world about Jesus.
Examples:
'From the sun's rising'
'Go forth and tell'
'From where the sun rises'
'He's got the whole world in his hands'
'As we see the world in tatters'
'This little light of mine'
'It only takes a spark'
'I want to serve the purpose of God'
'How lovely on the mountains'
'Tell all the world of Jesus'

Prayers

Praise

Select pairs of couplets from this responsive prayer of praise, making sure to include ones that your congregation can identify with, and finishing with the last two.

Through the massive Asian spaces,
You are God through all the world.
All Africa's hidden places,
You are God through all the world.
Small New Zealand, vast Australia,
You are God through all the world.
All the Middle East, Arabia,
You are God through all the world.
Baltic States, the huge Pacific,
You are God through all the world.
Scotland, England, Wales (terrific!),
You are God through all the world.
China, Chile, Turkey, Thailand,
You are God through all the world.
Republic of and Northern Ireland,
You are God through all the world.
America - from coast to highlands,
You are God through all the world.
North and South and tiny islands,
You are God through all the world.
Europe's countryside and cities,
You are God through all the world.
Mongolia (wherever it is!),
You are God through all the world.
North and South Pole, frozen wastes,
You are God through all the world.
Not forgetting outer space,
You are God through all the world.
All the places we forgot,
You are God through all the world.
God most certainly has not!
You are God through all the world.

Prayer for mission workers

Capture the congregation's imagination for praying for a particular mission partner by arranging a live telephone link to another part of the world *during* the service. Suitable equipment would allow both sides of the conversation to be relayed through a sound system, but the absence of this technology will not diminish the impact of this event. The excitement is almost as great if the leader of the service merely repeats to the congregation what he or she hears through the receiver. Ask the person on the other end of the telephone for the most up-to-date news about his or her work, and what the congregation should pray for at this moment. Follow the phone call by praying for the things that the mission worker has mentioned.

Responding to God

Give everyone in the congregation a postcard. One side should be blank, and on the other should be written the full postal address of someone known to the church who has a missionary role and is working at a distance from the church. In the top right-hand corner (where the stamp goes) write the price of postage to that destination. (Having some stamps available of that value after the service would help people who might forget to buy the correct stamp later!) If several people are supported or known by the church, offer a choice of cards.

Invite everyone, either individually or in families or friendship groups, to take the postcard home. They should make a point of praying for the missionary whose name and address is on the card - it doesn't matter if they don't know much about him or her, because God knows all there is to know! They should then write a note on the blank side of the card, explaining what they have been praying. Alternatively, they could draw a picture as a present for the person. During the week, put the correct stamp on it and send it. Imagine the encouragement these people will have when a heap of mail arrives assuring them of our prayers!

Words of self-offering

A prayer of Mother Teresa of Calcutta:

Here I am, Lord - body, heart and soul;
Grant that, with your love,
I may be big enough to reach the world,
And small enough to be at one with you.
Amen.

christian life

OUTLINE 40

SERVICE THEME
God gives us gifts of creativity

CHRISTIAN THEME
The Christian life

BIBLE BASE
Exodus 31:1–11

ALL-AGE SERVICE SUMMARY
An opportunity to recognise and affirm people who use creative and artistic gifts to enhance worship and to give everyone an opportunity to use their own creative gifts to praise God.

THIS WEEK'S RESOURCES
Choose at least one active way for all the congregation to use creativity. This will help those who feel that God has not given them creative gifts to recognise that he has!

Setting the scene

If you worship in a room which has beautiful objects in it, such as stained-glass windows, pictures, furniture, banners and so on, talk about them to the congregation. Talk about their history, their meaning and the reason for having beautiful things in your church building. If you worship in a plainer room, bring in a piece of craft work which is designed to bring glory to God. Read Luke 21:5 to show that Jesus' disciples were glad to worship in a place which had been made beautiful in God's honour. But where does all this creativity come from? In today's service, we will find out!

Bible reading
Exodus 31:1–11

To make this reading more accessible, have two people to represent Bezalel and Oholiab coming to stand at the front near the reader as they are mentioned. Bezalel should carry a bag from which is unpacked some of the following: rolls of paper, a gold, silver or bronze article, carved wood. Oholiab could have a large picture of the 'tabernacle' or some of the articles mentioned, drapes of rich-looking fabric and a stone flask. The reader should pause while the items are unpacked and displayed.

Bible teaching for all ages

The talk falls into five sections:
1 Introduce the concept of the Holy Spirit giving gifts.
2 Explain what the tabernacle was and why it was important that Bezalel and Oholiab (Exodus 31:1–11) should be filled with the Holy Spirit to enable them to be artistic. The work had to be their very best, just as God had instructed.
3 Talk about the items they made to bring glory to God, the pure gold lamp stand, table and its articles, altar of incense, and priest's garments.
4 Compare this with the way people in your own congregation work artistically to glorify God through the Spirit's power. Give examples at adult and at child level, of ways in which members of your church contribute creatively to God's worship.
5 Do something creative together in praise of God, such as the 'Be artistic!' activity.

Ideas for music

Choose songs and hymns celebrating the gifts that the Holy Spirit has made available and our relationship through Jesus to the Creator God. Examples:

'Angel voices ever singing'
Come to us, creative Spirit'
'From you all skill and science flow'
'Our God is one who makes things'
'Praise God from whom all blessings flow'
'Who paints the skies into glorious day?'
'I am fearfully and wonderfully made'
'Lord, you've put a tongue in my mouth'
'Praise God in his holiness'
Praise the Lord in the rhythm of your music'
'We are being built into a temple'
'We are one body in the Lord'

Prayers

Creative movement

Ask a group to present the song, 'Open our eyes, Lord' with simple movements. Get the group to teach these to the congregation so that they may praise God creatively with their bodies as well as their voices:

Open our eyes, Lord *(hands touch eyes)*,
We want to see Jesus *(open eyes and stretch hands forward)*,
To reach out and touch him,
And say that we love him *(lift hands above head and then open palms)*,
Open our ears, Lord,
And help us to listen *(touch ears)*,
Open our eyes, Lord *(stretch out arms across those of neighbours)*,
We want to see Jesus *(look around at others in the room and smile!)*.

Commissioning

Ask all the groups who regularly contribute the Spirit's creative gifts to the church's worship to stand one at a time - the flower arrangers, the choir, the cleaners, the instrumentalists, the drama or dance groups, the artists, etc. Pray for them and commission them in God's service for the next year.

Be artistic!

Give each member of the congregation, young and old alike, a square of coloured paper. They fold it in half, then in half again (into a square), then across a diagonal (into a triangle). They tear small pieces from the edges, and open it to show a beautiful pattern. Ask them to show each other the results, and to put the scraps of paper in their pockets, not on the floor!

Then take an offering, in which they may give their artwork to God. When the papers have been collected, the leader should lift them before God with a dedicatory prayer. A few families may like to spend time later arranging the squares into a patchwork pattern on a wall in the room, a communal piece of creativity by the church of God.

Prayers of intercession

Praise God for the beauty of his creation. Ask that we may use, not waste, the gifts the Holy Spirit gives us. Pray against the abuse of creativity through pornography or propaganda.

remembrance

remembrance

EXTRA!
Remembrance Sunday

RESOURCES
This page contains individual ideas to be used for a service of remembrance when all ages are together. They are not intended to be used in a single act of worship.

An act of remembrance

This prayer is for two voices with a congregational response. Voice 1 reads words from Scripture: Lamentations 3:22,23; Romans 8:38; John 11:25; 1 Thessalonians 4:14.

Voice 1: 'The steadfast love of the Lord never ceases.'

Voice 2: Thank you, Lord, for your great love for us. Hold us in that love now and evermore.
Strengthen our faith, Lord.

Voice 1: 'I am sure that neither death, nor life … nor things present, nor things to come … will be able to separate us from the love of God in Christ Jesus our Lord.'

Voice 2: Thank you, Lord, for your great love for us. Hold us in that love now and evermore.
Strengthen our faith, Lord.

Voice 1: Jesus says, 'I am the resurrection and the life. Whoever believes in me, even though they die, will live.'

Voice 2: Thank you, Lord, for the life you offer us. Bring us to fullness of life now and evermore.
Strengthen our faith, Lord.

Voice 1: 'For since we believe that Jesus died and rose again, even so, through Jesus, God will bring with him those who have died.'

Voice 2: Thank you, Lord, for the life you offer us. Bring us to fullness of life now and evermore.
Strengthen our faith, Lord.

Voice 1: Loving and living God, we remember before you now all those whom we have loved and who are no longer with us. Grant them, with us, peace where there will be no mourning, crying or pain. Amen.

War 'games'

Ask those who play computer games to describe some of those which they enjoy playing. Inevitably, many of them will be based on war or battle themes. Point out that real war, the sort you are remembering today, is not at all like that. It means difficulty, pain, suffering and death for many, many ordinary people. Cite a few current examples which show that war is not about soldiers enjoying fighting, but means that normal life no longer exists for anyone in the war zone. Remind the congregation that those whose names are remembered today were loved by their families and friends, so many people were affected when they were killed. Part of our remembrance should be to think about all who suffer because of war. We also need to pray that God will show us how to put an end to war for ever.

Remembering

In advance, ask members of the congregation who are old enough to remember the Second World War to be interviewed about their memories. According to their situation, ask them how they felt when they (or a member of their family) were called up to fight; what good memories they have from wartime; what was their experience of being evacuated or bombed; what changes came about because of rationing; whether they knew anyone who died or was injured in wartime. Ask those who have no wartime memories of their own to remember what they have heard during the act of remembrance.

A field of poppies

Discuss the red poppies that are worn on and around Remembrance time, explain the reasons for this custom and that money raised from the sale of the poppies is used to help care for people (and their families) who have fought in the wars. Make sure that everyone has a poppy (bought purpose-made or made from circles of red paper and flexible drinking straws). After the act of remembrance and the minute's silence, as a way of expressing what they have been thinking about, invite those who wish to do so to come forward and push their poppy into a large piece of florist's arrangement block (Oasis). Conclude by praying for those who still have sad thoughts and memories and for those who long for peace in today's world.

An acrostic poem

P for the poppies we all wear
with pride.
E for the enemy we need to forgive.
A for the anger we lay on one side.
C is for Christ in the place where
we live.
E is for everyone learning to grow.
PEACE is the way God helps us
to go.

Laying a wreath

Ask those who normally lay a wreath on behalf of the church to allow one or two children to accompany them. As a symbolic way of passing on the duty to remember to the next generations, they could carry the wreath forward and solemnly hand it over to the children to lay at the memorial.